Additional Praise for *Finding Our Way to the Truth*

"This is one of those rare books that feels more like a conversation with the author than printed words on a page. By weaving her story throughout her book, Sarah addresses the seven lies that leaders believe. This approach not only held my attention, it also solidified the insights and learning that Sarah offers. This book is a definite read for today's leaders."
—J. Val Hastings, Master Certified Coach, president and founder of Coaching4Today'sLeaders and Coaching 4Clergy

"*Finding Our Way to the Truth* calls us to honest self-reflection. Sarah Ciavarri's beautiful writing helps us expose the lies that lead us away from living authentically. Full of stories and inspiring wisdom, this book will help you address the falsehoods that keep you from more fully making a difference in the world."
—Lois Malcolm, The Olin and Amanda Fjelstad Reigstad Chair of Systematic Theology, Luther Seminary

"These days, a pastor's job is made more difficult by shrinking churches and tighter budgets. Yet, healthy pastoral leadership, the kind that knits communities together in the love of Christ, is more necessary than ever. Into this world of disposable relationships, easy violence and broken institutional systems, Sarah casts a mature vision for healthy spiritual leaders. By exposing us to the unconscious lies that play like a broken record in our

minds, Sarah captures some of the greatest internal struggles every pastor endures and trains us to risk leading in challenging times. (book title) is delightfully full of wry insight, masterful storytelling, refreshing humor and brave encouragement. I highly recommend this refreshing guide to anyone searching for inspiration and tools to navigate the tough terrain of pastoral leadership in our time."
—The Rev. Sherry Cothran, Pastor, St. Mark's UMC, Chattanooga, TN

"Sarah clearly articulates through stories, struggles, and the joys of her own relationships how important it is to realize that there is no shame in the realization that 'I am enough.' Through her own vulnerability and transparency with humor, compassion, and boldness, Sarah points out that we are created in the image of a loving God, and there is no shame in that. As we take this journey, it leads us to the realization that the more we accept the reality of grace in our life and who God has created us to uniquely be, the more we grow as a leader, spouse, parent, friend, and servant. This book will make you laugh, make you cry, and most importantly, lead you in grace to overwhelming joy in the truth that 'I am enough.' It is wonderful launching point for personal and spiritual growth. Thank you, Sarah, for such a grace-filled journey!"
—Bob Mooney, senior pastor, Messiah Lutheran Church, Yorba Linda, CA

"A must-read for leaders! Sarah's authenticity and vulnerability leave you with practical applications for leadership and life. Her stories draw you in and keep you engaged. Inspiring, motivating, and thought-provoking!"
—Barb Schwery, Executive Director, BeFriender Ministry

"*Finding Our Way to the Truth* beautifully entwines story and deep reflections to inspire a new vision for embracing our authentic selves. Ciavarri eloquently describes how to be brave in confronting the lies that often plague our thoughts. This practical and compelling piece provides thought-provoking scenarios and ideas for cultivating authenticity while embracing our own truth. This is a powerful read for all, including educators, intentionally traveling down the path to cultivating communities of learning where students can bring and be their truest selves."
—Nicole M. Dimich, Educator, Author, and Consultant

"In this book Sarah Ciavarri has skillfully woven critical life questions with her personal experience in a manner that invites me into the conversation and leaves me asking, 'What does this mean for me? For those I love or serve?' What a wonderful tool for helping reframe the unhelpful messages that too often dominate our inner landscape."
—The Rev. Jim Gonia, Bishop, Rocky Mountain Synod, Evangelical Lutheran Church in America

Finding Our Way to the Truth

Finding Our Way to the Truth

Seven Lies Leaders Believe and How to Let Go of Them

Sarah Ciavarri

FORTRESS PRESS
MINNEAPOLIS

FINDING OUR WAY TO THE TRUTH
Seven Lies Leaders Believe and How to Let Go of Them

Scripture quotations are from the New Revised Standard Version Bible © 1989 Division of Christian Education of the National Council of the Churches of Christ in the United States of America. Used with permission.

Some names and identifying details have been changed to protect the privacy of individuals.

Cover Design and Illustration: Brad Norr Design

Print ISBN: 978-1-5064-5658-4

Ebook ISBN: 978-1-5064-5660-7

To my parents, Ron and DiAnn Jacobson, for roots and wings.

Contents

Preface   xiii

Acknowledgments   xv

Foreword   xvii
N. Graham Standish

1. Truth and Lies   1
2. "I Don't Know Enough"   7
   Honesty
3. "I Must Finish What I Start"   19
   Moderation
4. "I Must Follow the Rules"   35
   Discernment
5. "I Have to Be Nice"   51
   Boundaries
6. "People Must Like Me"   67
   Integrity
7. "I'm Responsible for It All"   83
   Hope
8. "I Need to Be the Right Type of Christian"   97
   Authenticity
9. An Invitation   115

Preface

When Beth Gaede, a senior editor for Fortress Press, invited me to have a conversation about the possibility of writing a book, I was not going to overpromise. My go-to behavior for years was to say "Yes!" to every opportunity that came my way and then figure out how to deliver. But let's be honest: Even though I imagined it would be cool to casually drop in conversation, "Oh, yeah, I'm writing a book," the oohs and aahs that might garner would not be reward enough for the hours spent writing and rewriting, praying, "God, give me words that are worth people's time to read."

When we visited over lunch several weeks later, I practiced a new but very freeing behavior: I was very up-front about my limitations. I told her that I didn't know if I could write a book, and that if I could, it wouldn't be a deeply academic one containing five-syllable words you'd need to (1) be a subject matter insider to understand or (2) flip to the glossary to decode. I said my gift was in telling stories, and I wasn't sure there'd be enough to make a book out of. Furthermore, writing a book wasn't on my radar. I told her the story of getting ready that morning to speak at a gathering for pastors and deacons later that day, and out of the blue I'd scowled and said to no one but God and my reflection in the mirror, "Yu-uck! Who'd ever want to write a book? Yu-UCK!" Three hours later, she approached me to ask if I'd like to talk about writing a book.

This came completely out of nowhere!

Beth and I laughed about my morning revelation and wondered about it. What was God possibly doing? I shared again that I didn't know if I could write a book, but if it was something God was doing, I'd keep showing up and trying. Beth said several times, "I think there might be a book here. Let's keep going until we know there isn't." We left our lunch with next steps in mind.

If I had overpromised, I would have believed this book came to be because I "sold" Fortress Press on the idea of who I was—a "better," more confident version of myself—and I think you'd have a completely different book in your hands, one that would read like I was trying to convince you of something. Instead of writing to persuade, I offer you an invitation to explore the impact of lies—lies such as "People must like me" and "I must be nice"—in your life as I explore them in mine. I was honest with my limitations.

I told Beth that I didn't know if I could write a book, but if it was God's work, I would keep showing up and keep trying. I could easily and authentically commit to that. In the end, authenticity led the way. Even when my ideas weren't clear or the words wouldn't come and I spent twenty minutes rephrasing three sentences and then typed "blah, blah, f*ckety blah, blah," I can now happily share that "Yu-uck! Who'd ever want to write a book?" never crossed my lips again.

Acknowledgments

Thank you, Beth Gaede, for your expert and patient guidance as we "let the book reveal itself." What a gift! And to Fortress Press for seeking out new authors.

For ministry and healthcare colleagues, I say thanks be to God! To Rev. Lori Lathrop, you care for my soul so well. To Rev. Nancy Carlson, for believing in my work and for dreaming and praying visions into reality. To Cassia for saying yes to that vision. To Bishop Ann Svennungsen, Bishop Jim Gonia, Rev. Dr. David Lose, Dr. Lois Malcolm, Rev. Dr. Dawn Alitz and her staff at Faith+Lead, Concordia College leaders, and Don Richter and the Louisville Institute's Pastoral Study Project Grant, which provided encouragement and funding to support my work. To Dave Shaw and our leadership team at Augustana Health Care and Rehabilitation Center of Apple Valley and the Apple Valley Villa, for the gift of working with people I respect and genuinely enjoy. To those who attend workshops I lead: I'm so grateful for how you show up.

Thank you to Dr. Brené Brown and the Daring Way™ community—Brené, for the research that changed my life and the honor I have to bring that to leaders, and the Daring Way™ community, for being such an amazing group of people; inspiration abounds!

Thank you to the elders and their families whom I've had the blessing to learn from over the last twenty-five years; I live more intentionally because of you.

To the staff at my hometown Good Samaritan Center for all I learned from you and your love. Val Eide, Deb Melby, and the late Rev. Jerry Carlson: thank you for saying yes to a crazy idea God gave you.

Thank you to friends and extended family. To Spiritus and my Ship friends for laughter that has filled my soul for years. To college and seminary professors and friends, including Dr. Lace Williams-Tinajero: you are like my sister. To my godparents, Ron and Mary Alice Bergan, my gratitude is so deep: your quiet and steadfast support of my work means more than you know. To my godparents, the late Uncle Wally and Aunt Marlys Rustad, for your example of commitment to each other and family.

To my parents, Ron and DiAnn Jacobson: thank you for providing me opportunities to explore and develop my gifts and talents as a child and teen. The sacrifices you made out of love years ago will never be lost on me.

To my children: Chiara, who made amazing cookies and cakes to fuel me in the last weeks of writing this book, and Jacob, who was relieved when I said he didn't have to read this book. Chiara and Jacob, I am so glad to be *your* mama.

To my husband, Tim. When God brought us together, a world of blessings I had only dreamed of opened up. You are my home.

And to the Sustainer of all life, the Lord God, who gives the gift of time. May I use it well.

Foreword

N. Graham Standish

Being a pastor means feeling guilty—a lot! No matter how good our intentions, no matter how much we care and want to care, no matter how much we want to be there for others, we just aren't good enough.

If you believe this, then you really need to pay attention to what Sarah Ciavarri has to say, because it can heal some of your wounds. The reality is that pastoral ministry is guilt-inducing for pastors, but not because we aren't good enough. The truth is we aren't called to be everything for everyone. In congregations where everyone has so many different needs, we're called to nurture compassion, to engage in service and prayer, to be aware, to learn, to grow, and so much more, but there are limits to what we can do. When we exceed those limits, our lives start to falter. To be a pastor means to set limits as we grapple with a basic question: What has to give so that we can live as pastors who give?

I had a mentor, Father Adrian van Kaam, whom I studied with as part of my doctoral studies. He's the only genius I've ever met, and I've met a lot of really, really smart people. He wrote fifty-two books or more in his lifetime. In his writings and teachings, he integrated insights from spirituality, theology, philosophy, psychology, sociology, and so much more, but he did so all while still remaining one of the humblest people I've ever known. He had a combination of vast knowledge, deep understanding, and great wisdom that few manage to hold together. Through his focus on fostering a deeper spiritual life, he spoke to the problem of pastoral guilt, and of guilt in general, and how it relates to spiritual life.

He taught that we have to learn to distinguish between *psychological guilt* and *spiritual guilt.* Psychological guilt is a form of denigrating guilt that screams at us from the depths of our self-judgments and devaluations and our feelings of inadequacy, denigration, and diminishment. It's a guilt that weighs on us after a lifetime of hearing about how deficient we are and about how often we've failed. It's not necessarily a guilt rooted in reality; it's a guilt grounded in the negative memes constantly running through our heads that were bestowed upon us through a lifetime of listening to the criticisms and unrealistic expectations of others.

Spiritual guilt is different. It is a whispering guilt that often escapes our attention. It's rooted in God's love, reminding us that we are more than we think we are, and we have gifts we are barely aware of. It's a kind of guilt that comes from God, and it invites us to follow God's call to make life better for others and for ourselves. Spiritual guilt is God's hushed voice telling us that there's another way to respond to life, and if we listen, follow, and take action, it will be life-giving and life-affirming. This guilt isn't always tied to our vocation, and it often whispers a different message than what psychological guilt screams at us. We hear the voice of spiritual guilt as we hush the nagging yelps of other kinds of guilt and settle in to hear what God is actually calling us to do. The problem is that because psychological guilt's emotional deluge often drowns out spiritual guilt, it usually becomes the only guilt we respond to.

Psychological guilt tells us to do more so that people will like us more, so that people will give us accolades (or at least stop giving us condemnations), so that we can be deemed a success. Psychological guilt doesn't care about our personal lives, our familial lives, or our spiritual lives unless it attaches itself to one of these, causing us to feel guilty over our inability to do better in our personal, familial, and spiritual lives. Ultimately, psychological guilt eats away at us. Spiritual guilt nourishes us because it connects us with God's call. It guides us by softly telling us that there's a better way of living, of being, and of serving in ministry. It's a way that allows God's Spirit and grace to flow through us.

Why am I going on and on about these two kinds of guilt? Because this book offers a crucial step in disconnecting us from the more destructive kind of guilt while opening us up to the more affirming kind of guilt that comes from God and that gently nudges us to a more holy, healthy, and healing way.

Sarah Ciavarri offers us a more nurturing path toward listening to God's voice by encouraging us to become more honest with ourselves. Through story, metaphor, and life lessons, she explores the kinds of things we already know about ourselves but are rarely willing to explore. She helps us take the time to get to know ourselves, and through this, to know what our true callings are in ministry. She helps us uncouple from the shackling guilt that slowly drags us down by helping us be honest enough to be able to say, "I want to hear what helps me to heal and be a healer."

Each chapter wonderfully explores the different kinds of guilt-inducing, self-destructive, lying memes we tell ourselves that keep us from flourishing. It's not always the bad lies that hurt us. Sometimes the good ones hurt, too, because they tap into a false sense of reality that keeps us from being honest with ourselves and with our calling.

As I read this book, it took me back to an experience

I had years ago as a church pastor during a time when we began to attract younger families. With so many young children running around the church, and with their parents lamenting to me that they often felt inadequate, several suggested we offer parenting classes. "What a great idea," I thought. I had been trained in parenting skills through my work with children as a therapist. I knew the value of these classes. So I found a person trained in a parenting program who would be willing to offer a six-week set of sessions on Thursday evenings. We hoped for at least ten couples to sign up. We got four. Discouragingly, the parents who asked for the classes never showed. Afterward, I followed up with them and asked why they never signed up. Their answer: "I was worried that the teacher might tell me that I'm a bad parent. I just couldn't take that." So they stayed away from a course that would help them become good parents because of the fear that they might be labeled bad parents. Destructive lies and memes hold us back. Sarah gently encourages us to let those destructive lies and memes go so that we can more forward.

She offers wonderful, gently crafted insights that can really help us become more authentic so we can let go of harmful lies that tell us we are inadequate in order to hear how God is calling us to be pastors. These are insights such as, "This process for living more authentically isn't once and done; this is lifelong work," or "The key is finding someone we can be honest and authentic with when we feel that our safest bet is to hide and pretend—someone who will say, 'There is always more to learn, and that's okay. Bring what you've got and lead, anyway,'" or "Setting and maintaining life-giving boundaries isn't a once-and-done deal. It is a lifelong task that begins with self-awareness—knowing what is going on in our emotions, thoughts, and behaviors."

What I really value in Sarah's work is her gentleness. I'm tempted to say that in a very NICE way, she explores how to be honest and discerning, boundary-setting and balanced, vulnerable and authentic, but that might get me in trouble in Minnesota (as you'll discover). A better way of saying it is that Sarah uses a very KIND approach to help us forge healthier approaches to ministry, leadership, pastoral care, and community-building.

I hope you find this book as helpful as I have.

The Rev. N. Graham Standish, PhD, MSW, MA, MDiv.

Author of . . . *And the Church Actually Changed: Uncommon Wisdom for Pastors in the Age of Doubt, Division, and Decline* and *Becoming a Blessed Church: Forming a Church of Spiritual Purpose, Presence, and Power.* https://www.ngrahamstandish.org

1.

Truth and Lies

Have you ever played the "Two Truths and a Lie" icebreaker game? Each player takes a turn sharing three statements about themselves with the group. Two statements are true, and one is a lie. The object of the game is to figure out which is the lie. Sometimes it is really obvious which one is the lie, because—if you are playing with someone like our ten-year-old son, Jacob—when they tell the lie, they start laughing while saying, "I'm serious!" Other times, the lies seem so believable or the truths so outlandish that you are duped. The more sophisticated the acting skills, the harder it is to tell truth from fiction.

Truth and Lies isn't just a game we play when friends come over or at a family reunion. In very subtle ways, we play it every day when we think about ourselves, our situation, our future. It gets hard to tell the difference sometimes between truth and lies. Lies masquerading as truths can be so engrained in how we were raised, the culture we live in, or what type of thinking has kept us safe that we don't notice when one has just informed our decisions. And these decisions have impacts on how we lead, work, parent, and live.

The lies we are going to look at in this book aren't the obvious ones. We are looking at sneaky ones. They are sneaky because we could say about each of these lies, "But that's good, that's true, isn't it? That's how it works." Yes, to a point. These lies can be benign, even helpful, perhaps in limited situations for limited periods of time. But when we make these lies into absolutes and dig into actual stories from our lives, we see their limitations and, in turn, how they have limited our lives. Maybe they've kept us from owning our ideas or strengths, from following a dream, from confronting dysfunction, from enjoying deeper, more honest relationships.

These are the lies we will take on in this book:

- I don't know enough.
- I must finish what I start.
- I must follow the rules.
- I have to be nice.
- People must like me.
- I'm responsible for it all.
- I need to be the right type of Christian.

This is not an exhaustive list of all the slimy lies we tell ourselves, but looking at these will give us a good start at developing awareness, hitting pause, and reflecting on what is happening. Then we can change our thinking so we feel better about ourselves and can live with more intention, calm, and authenticity. We will do this through a three-step process you'll find at the end of each chapter:

Pay Attention

Think about how an experienced mountaineer identifies how fresh animal tracks are, what the weather is doing, and where the best place is to cross a river: he or she pays attention to the environment, constantly reading the situation and their own responses to it. In order to track down lies we hold as true, we need to become like that expedition guide. We need to pay attention not only to what the environment is telling us, but to what is going on inside of us. We will want to be able to answer these questions when we are on the trail of a sneaky lie:

- What are my thoughts?
- What are my actions in relation to others' actions?
- What is my physical response to situations? When does my gut tighten? What situations make my heart race? Why is that?

This first step is simply to be aware.

Examine

Once we know a lie is leading us away from our real inner self—our authentic being—we need to examine it. We can do this by ourselves through an exercise like journaling, or we can talk it out with someone we trust. Either way, we start probing the lie by asking more questions to see whether the lie perhaps isn't as true or universal as we first thought. We ask questions like these:

- Is this thought actually true? When else has this been true? When hasn't this thought been true? What do my previous experiences teach me?
- How will I feel about myself if I follow this thought? What consequences might I experience?

- If I don't follow this thought, what might happen?

Most of us weren't schooled in this technique of reflective examination and may wonder if this is a sign of being stuck—ruminating or perseverating about a situation. I have been in that quagmire many times (and I know I will be again!)—when my thoughts are stuck replaying an event in my mind and I'm rehearsing really awesome comebacks to a statement made three weeks or years before. Honestly, I *just* came up with a really good comeback for an argument that happened . . . fifteen months ago.

Reflective examination is different from rumination, though. Ruminating keeps us stuck; reflective examination has the power to get us unstuck. In reflective examination, we bring a spirit of calm and kindness to our thinking. We hold the intent of learning about ourselves, others, and the situation so we can make choices that are more life-giving and truer for us in the future.

Apply the Learning

Now that a lie is exposed, what truth is revealed? Now that you know something you didn't before, what will this new insight mean for you? What shift might you make the next time this lie sneaks up? In this step, we explore what the new insight means and how we can integrate it into our lives. Integration happens when we change our thoughts and behaviors because we are aware they don't serve us well.

For example, I used to apologize excessively; I'd bump into someone on the escalator—"Sorry!" I couldn't get the slides switched in a PowerPoint presentation fast enough—"Sorry!" I've been paying attention to my profuse apologizing for over fifteen years, and I've gotten 90 percent better by catching when I say it, thinking about situations I often encounter when I'm likely to say it unnecessarily, and then intentionally replacing it with other phrases or even a silent pause. The truth I learned is to be grounded, not smaller or bigger than I truly am. That's integration.

This process for living more authentically isn't once and done; this is lifelong work. "Sorry!" still comes unintentionally skidding out of my mouth when I'm hyper-focused on a worry, when I'm irritated, or when I'm tired. We are constantly learning and growing, integrating new understandings that expand a previous insight or point us in an entirely new direction. But when that learning happens, not only is it good for *us*, but then we have more to offer those we love and lead. This integration work is hard—but it's worth it because it helps us feel better about ourselves, more whole and complete. The new insights are like mind candy and soul food. They are like a nutrient-rich dish we bring to the relationship potluck.

It's Time to End the Game

I think lots of us are ready to stop playing Truth and Lies; we just have too many other things we'd rather do in our lives. Playing this game siphons an untold amount of joy and fulfillment from serving as a pastor, leading a school, being a solopreneur, raising a family, caring for patients. So many people across numerous fields tell me that their work isn't as much fun as it used to be. They don't feel as connected to the mission, to their colleagues, or even to the belief that their work makes a difference as they used to feel. And making a difference was a primary motivation for choosing their particular career. They daydream about doing something better or more meaningful while scrolling through job-posting sites—there are days you'll find me scrolling, too.

The lies we will look at in the following chapters don't just show up in our work, though. They are everywhere we go, because they've gotten attached to us on a deeper level, a soul level, and that is what makes them so dangerous. They can strangle the life out of us long before we die and replace a sense of well-being and hope with regret and resentment.

I believe that God wants better for us, that we were created for better, and that we do better for the world when we stop playing Truth and Lies. The intent of this book is to help us find a sense of well-being and hope again, even when the game beckons us back for just one more round.

2.

"I Don't Know Enough"
Honesty

Back in the era of big hair and big shoulder pads, of tightly rolling up the hem of your jeans even if you froze your ankles in winter, I was in college. One day my mom called me at school and said, "The Good Sam"—shorthand for a large local senior residence run by the Good Samaritan Society—"wants you to be the chaplain this summer." Where did this come from? My résumé for religious work included two summers as a Bible camp counselor, a work-study position as secretary in the campus pastors' office, serving as a listener at the church I attended in college and . . . being nice.

"Do they know I've had only two classes in religion?"

"Yes, and they want you to do it anyway."

Huh. I never saw that coming.

So, for three summers I drove five miles from my parents' farm into town to the nursing home. I had never been a chaplain, I wasn't trained for this work, and I didn't know enough. If I had walked into a care center anyplace else and applied to be a chaplain, I would not even have gotten an interview. But not knowing enough didn't limit how I showed up at the nursing home. I just showed up and prayed my way through every day.

The setting wasn't completely unfamiliar. Before I was in school, back when I spent my days trailing behind my

7

dad on the farm and going to Grandma and Grandpa's house for afternoon coffee (they lived right next door), my grandma had taken my older brother and me to sing "Jesus Loves Me" and "Jesus Wants Me for a Sunbeam" for my Great-Grandma Selma, who lived in the Good Sam. She was a stoic woman with Norwegian ancestry, a woman who had come to North Dakota from Iowa, leaving behind the fertile fields for the windswept prairie, a hope, and a dream. She'd married my Great-Grandpa Henry, and like most pioneers, they had carved out a life on the 160 acres they homesteaded.

The remnants of those early days were still visible. The old threshing machine sat behind our barn in the pigpen, an old rusted plow was being reclaimed by prairie grass in the shelter belt, and the old Model T Ford pickup was parked next to the granary, convenient for the mice who had eaten their fill of wheat and seat cushions. These reminders of a harder life were our playground as kids; we'd crawl into the belly of the threshing machine or pretend we were driving the old Model T. Like the life of all pioneers, my great-grandma's was one of hard work, long hours, and seemingly endless winters. When the Good Samaritan Center opened in 1968, she was the first person to move in. After all that hard work, the "rest home," as it was called then—where other people cooked your meals and other people did your laundry and other people cleaned your toilet and other people were charged with making sure the living kept on—apparently was very attractive.

I went back to the Good Sam over the years as a Girl Scout, and then as a "candy-striper," calling bingo and replenishing water pitchers for residents in their rooms. I imagine my friends and I didn't take our candy-striping tasks as seriously as we should have. I imagine we were more interested in talking with each other than being a sunbeam for Jesus or any other form of light, spreading rays of love and service to the man slumped over in his wheelchair or the woman who was hard of hearing.

So it wasn't as if these halls were unknown to me when I returned with my big bangs and big shoulder pads in the early nineties, but I was entering a world in which I was on the edge of my skills, needing to trust more than know, pushing myself to do the uncomfortable things every day—to get out of my office and go knock on the room doors of residents and attempt to build trust, rapport, and a relationship with the simple, yet complicated, purpose of loving them.

Every morning I'd drive those five highway miles, maybe see one other car on the road, and arrive at this both familiar and foreign land. Any assumption that I should know more or that I didn't know enough was quickly silenced by the incredible invitation from the administrator to try, to learn, to fail, to grow. I learned that I loved being on the edge of my skill: I found I trusted the Holy Spirit more, I had to work through my fear, and I had to get used to the idea that I would do things every day that I hadn't done before. I preached, led Bible studies, launched an (ultimately unsuccessful) Alzheimer's caregivers support group.

When I did feel like I needed to be impressive or that I had to prove my worth, show I was competent, or "earn my keep"—that's when I fumbled things up. Like the time I thought a "Christmas in July" service would remind us all that Jesus comes to be with us all year and that the joy we feel at Christmas is something we carry year-round. While this theme may be a successful sales tactic to push ornaments in summer tourist traps, it was not the wisest of ideas in a nursing home. Where people live with dementia. Which means they may be disoriented to time of year and seasons. Which means setting up a Christmas tree and decorating it when it is 90 degrees outside and the sun doesn't set until 10 p.m. makes for a disorienting experience. And not very impressive.

The main thing I did, though, was listen to elders for hours a day. I was a story catcher. In catching these stories, I learned valuable lessons about leadership, like that we all want to be seen for what makes us unique. There was a woman who had loved to bowl in her younger years. In our first visit she talked about how much fun she had in a bowling league for nearly three decades. I got the idea of bringing in my mom's old bowling ball, and this woman gave me a bowling lesson. Even though the wheelchair she needed confined her now, she spent an hour with me, showing me proper hand placement and wrist twist. I saw her unique passions that day.

A second leadership lesson came while I sat with a man who was visiting his mother-in-law with his wife as he recounted an incredible, harrowing story of bravery from World War II. With tears streaming down his face, he talked for two hours about torments you can't even imagine and about human decency that makes one deeply proud. He concluded by saying, "We just got busy living when we returned from the war. We didn't look back but built our families. I've never told anyone this story before." And I got to be there. He taught me an incredible lesson about serving those you lead.

I remember a bachelor farmer who had lived a hard, unjust life. He didn't believe in God. Repeatedly, in a gruff voice, he'd say, "The Bible is just a book of fairy tales." I didn't try to argue him into belief or quote him into conversion. I didn't offer to pray for him. Even though he scared me, I simply showed up—again and again and again—once wearing a floral Hawaiian dress and a plastic lei, carrying my "boom box" and a tape of Hawaiian songs to bring some joy and fun into his half of the room—because years before, he had taken a dream vacation to the Big Island. As I got ready to return to college that fall, in our final goodbye he said, "Behave. And I'll be praying for you." Taking risks to connect with someone else may feel foolish, and we may be rejected, but pushing through the fear just might lead us to rich blessings of seeing how God works.

I didn't hear these stories of tenacity and draw leadership lessons out of them because I knew enough. I heard these stories and learned from them simply because I showed up, which makes my mom's answer to my question, "Do they know I've had only two classes in religion?," even more profound. "Yes, and they want you to do it *anyway*." The nursing home leaders wanted me to spend the summer with them not because of my stellar résumé or proven work experience. What was on paper didn't matter. What did matter was that they saw my gifts before I did and graciously provided opportunities for me to try them out in a place where I received lots of autonomy to trust my gut, as well as lots of support and affirmation that it was okay to need help from time to time.

I experienced one of the gifts of growing up in a small community. It was just as natural for people in this part of the world to grow leaders as to grow flax, barley, and durum wheat. The nursing home administrator and director of nursing wanted me there because they believed in trying new things, in saying, "Why not?"—because those risks just might serve their mission. They blew the lie that we should know more right out of the water.

"And they want you to do it anyway."

In this simple response, my mom gave me a whole new take on the word "anyway." The word *anyway* is often used in western North Dakota culture as a transition word. It is time to leave a friend's dinner, and as a guest pushes her chair back from the table, she says, "Well, anyway, we should be going." It softens—or excuses—what is coming next. "This report isn't even going to be read, but we have to do it anyway." "I can't get these numbers to match up, so what do we do anyway?" *Anyway* certainly isn't a power word.

But that is what it has become for me. Over the years, that word *anyway* has taken on a holy meaning. *Anyway* acknowledges my limitations, assuring me I don't have to hide them, and it gives me permission to ask questions, to be honest, to not try to be more than I am. It says, "This doesn't make sense, you're scared, you're not supposed to do this, but do it anyway!"

"I don't want to put this project out there in the world—people can be so mean—but I'm going to do it anyway."

"This move doesn't make sense on paper, but because our children will be closer to grandparents, it feels right, so we're doing it anyway."

"We'll probably fail, but let's try anyway."

"It may not matter to others, but I'm going to live with intention anyway."

Anyway, for me, is this beautiful invitation to dance with what I have, to bring my whole self to leadership and to work, to remain grounded in my values and intentions, and to be supported by people who see my potential and want to bring out the best in me. And I want to do that for other people, so the lie that we should know more than we do doesn't make us want to hide what we don't know. Instead, we can say, "There is more to know. I'm going to learn it. I'm going to ask my questions. And I'm going to try this, anyway."

Throughout the years since I was a chaplain in my hometown nursing home, I haven't always lived with this sense of permission to be authentic. I can't tell you how many times "You should know more" whispers in my ear, warning me to be quiet. And I can't tell you how many times I listen. This has prevented me from learning new things or gaining a new perspective. When I don't ask questions in a meeting or when I'm presenting, it might be because I'm listening to the lie that I should already know something.

I suspect, though, that I'm not alone in listening to this lie. As a pastor who coaches other pastors, I know from our conversations about adult faith formation that parishioners buying into this lie is a reason many of them don't come to Bible study. "I should know more about the Bible than I do" keeps people from coming to the very place where they could learn more! Or this lie might be lurking in the background when a congregation is continually looking for lectors, people to read the Scripture lessons in worship, and potential readers don't come forward because they worry they don't know how to say unfamiliar four-syllable names from the book of Numbers. Or when a church meeting is about to start and the pastor is sick and participants wonder who will pray to open the meeting because people think they don't know enough about how to pray aloud. Finally, this lie might be slinking around when it is time to make a decision about a building project, a capital campaign, closing the church's preschool, or separating the governance of the church and the preschool . . . because even though feasibility studies have been prepared and focus groups have been held in prayer, just one more study would help us feel less vulnerable about stepping out in trust and trying a new approach to ministry, or taking a risk that supports the mission. I suspect this lie is at work when we pull back from hard conversations about social topics or challenging family dynamics—because we'd like to know more, think we should know more, and have it all figured out before we engage.

Furthermore, the lie that we should know more is alive and well in situations where our lack of knowledge is evident and we can't pretend or hide it, and people use that as a reason to gossip, tease, or belittle us, planting seeds of self-doubt. I remember grocery shopping one day and running into a man I'd known casually. In my previous interactions with him, he had occasionally lamented that people didn't read their Bibles more. We exchanged some small talk, and then he said, "I have a question for you. I've asked everyone this question, and nobody knows the right answer."

Dang, it's quiz time in the canned vegetable aisle. Just getting through this shopping trip was going to be more of a test than getting my first "real" job at the Good Sam.

"How many fish were there in the miraculous catch of fish?"

Whew! A question I knew the answer to: "One hundred fifty-three."

He responded, "That's right. But you *should* know that, because you're a pastor."

As I waited in the checkout lane, I realized this question had felt a bit adversarial. I also felt like having the right answer eliminated negative judgment he might have otherwise leveled at me. He wasn't expressing happiness that he learned something new about the Bible or sharing a story about what God had done in his life. He had quizzed other people, and they had all failed his quiz. It seemed to me at the time that if I hadn't known the correct answer, I would have given him ammunition to tease me for having less biblical knowledge than he did—and I had gone to seminary! I could easily imagine him using my incorrect answer to prove his point—that we need to read our Bibles more—the next time he got on a roll. And I might begin to believe it myself. If I felt shame in not knowing the correct answer and believed that I should know more, I might behave in ways that wouldn't serve my ministry well—quoting chapter and verse in a meeting, puffing up with my theology. And when I saw him again, I would try to avoid him or at least put up my defenses, which would prevent any real connection from happening. I agree with him that as a pastor I do need to be studying the Scriptures. But not for the purpose of correctly answering a quiz in the grocery store to avoid judgment.

Finding My Way to Truth: Honesty

As leaders, many of us are in positions laden with responsibilities and new initiatives that continue to expand. We can't possibly know everything before we need to know it. And just as a manager moving from a local to a regional position or a pastor serving a church that has grown in members learns, the leader's perspective must expand from the granular and detailed to the bigger picture and longer horizon. Even as the view changes, though, we can continually cultivate honesty about our limitations so we thrive in whatever environment we are in.

We find what is authentic when we pause, process, and reflect on our experiences. Were they life-giving? Did I behave in ways I feel good about? Did I treat other people well? Was I treated well? Is there a universal truth in this for me? A life lesson I can carry with me into other experiences? There is potential for great learning in every situation, if we have eyes to see it. The process of paying attention, examining, and applying the learning described in Chapter 1 is intended to help us do just that.

Pay Attention

Paying attention takes me back to my emotions, thoughts, and actions, both when things went well and when they went poorly. When my mom called with the invitation from Good Sam, the feeling I experienced was wonder: *I never would have imagined this! Wow! This is pretty crazy!* And I love surprises, so I saw the invitation as the beginning of an adventure. I immediately understood it as God's call and God's action; like the faithful who have gone before me, I just needed to say yes and go. By the grace of God, that is exactly what I did.

Examine

Upon reflection, I think my question, "Do they know I've only had two classes in religion?," was my first step into honesty. Even in this initial call, I wasn't going to overpromise; I wanted them to know exactly what I brought: *two* classes in religion. That's it. Not to mention, this happened in my small hometown. You could think of teen years in a small town as a very long job interview; they already knew the good, the bad, and the ugly about me!

The fact that I experienced my mom's phone call as a call from God leads me to understand several of the call stories in Scripture a bit differently. From Moses to Zechariah to Mary, we have framed their initial responses as doubt. Now I wonder, after my own experience, if they might also have felt a little desire to make sure God knew who they really were . . . to not overpromise to the Divine.

Knowing the Good Samaritan Center really did know who they were getting, I felt encouraged to be honest, pushing against the lie that I should know more.

Apply the Learning

I was uniquely blessed in this opportunity in that I wasn't expected to follow a lot of policies and procedures, so I could create and explore freely. I didn't feel much pressure to overpromise in an attempt to hide what I didn't know, and any pressure I did feel was of my own making.

But sometimes we do actually need to know more, and overpromising won't fill that gap. In that case, we fill the gap by learning from and working with mentors and colleagues who won't weaponize our lack of knowledge and use it against us, but who will help us grow. Unfortunately, not every work, family, or community environment is as supportive as the Good Samaritan Center was for me. The key is finding someone we can be honest and authentic with when we feel that our safest bet is to hide and pretend—someone who will say, "There is always more to learn, and that's okay. Bring what you've got and lead, anyway."

3.

"I Must Finish What I Start"

Moderation

Finishing what we start is important. Completing a project on time, on budget, and delivering what we said we would build trust with other people. It shows we are reliable and accountable. Like many of the lies I write about in this book, the notion that we must finish what we start is helpful to a point. But knowing when we have moved beyond that point is crucial, because carrying a principle too far can become destructive. It can prevent us from honestly and vulnerably admitting, "This project isn't going as planned. We need to pivot. We need to find another way." Or it can keep a pastor from observing, "I know we talked about this idea in the annual meeting, but no one is stepping up. I don't see much energy for it right now. Maybe this isn't what God is calling us to be about next." Or it can silence someone with a terminal illness from saying, "I don't want to keep on fighting." Many of us learned to finish what we started right along with our A-B-Cs and 1-2-3s.

If you walked into the cafeteria of the elementary school I attended back in the day, you'd first notice the wonderful smell of fresh-baked bread and home-cooked meals. You'd notice the milk dispenser with the big shiny metal bar you lifted up to let the milk flow into your glass. And you just might notice that at the end of the meal, students, one after another, showed their plates to the teacher on duty and asked if they could dump their tray. They were asking permission to be done eating. Sometimes our teachers, perhaps prompted by the fact that most of our parents made their living growing food for the world, would remind us when they spied scraps of Salisbury steak or rogue peas, that there were "starving children in Africa." And back we'd go to our long tables to finish up. Sometimes we'd be instructed to finish our carrots or to take three more bites of the canned peaches, much like we'd be told at the supper table back home hours later. By the time I reached the top of the elementary hierarchy in fifth grade, bread wasn't baked fresh every day and individual pint-sized milk cartons had replaced the shiny communal milk dispenser. We'd also learned a trick to save us from being sent back to the table to clean up our plates: we'd covertly fill our empty milk cartons with all the vegetables we didn't want to be guilted into eating.

The ritual in my family at our table, along with praying "Come, Lord Jesus" while holding hands, was to ask our parents if we could be excused when we were done eating. If you took too much of, say, eggplant and realized by trial and error that you weren't much of a fan, you'd learn to take less next time. Unless you were gagging, you still ate *all* the food in front of you. Food wasn't something you took for granted or wasted. Being a member of the clean-plate club was the goal of every farm kid of that generation. We came from people who had memories of the Depression, the Dirty Thirties, the Dust Bowl days when putting food on the table involved more tears and toil than we could imagine.

When I was a teenager, I started to disdain the fat on the edge of my porkchop or chunk of chuck roast. My father's typical assessment of my neat pile of gelatinous fat was to declare, "You are leaving the best part!" But that wasn't going to get me to eat it, no sirree! Refusing to eat the fat was my teenage rebellion, so he'd utter with dismay, "Give it here, I'll eat it." And in two bites, down went the best part.

Or the worst.

Depending on your perspective.

Whether it was school lunch, a novel you found boring, a football game in which you'd sustained a concussion, or something as significant as a loveless marriage, we learned from what people told us and what we saw—who was judged and for what they were judged—that you finish what you start and that there is no honor in quitting.

While succeeding was important, finishing what you started was about one's character. When I gave the high jump a try in high school, I quickly learned I wasn't going to sail over the bar like my older brother, so I would plow into it or run away from it, out of fear of falling on it. After one track meet, my mom and I celebrated because it was the first time I didn't quit. I scratched every time I jumped, knocking the bar off the uprights, but I didn't stop, I didn't quit, I didn't run away. We celebrated that more than the third-place finish I'd gotten in the 3,200-meter run. You finish what you start. Don't quit.

The first time my husband Tim met my family, he'd come to visit from New York. He had long hair and wore Grateful Dead T-shirts, handmade friendship bracelets, and Chuck Taylor sneakers. He had a degree in philosophy, and from all outward assessments, he was going nowhere fast in his dancing-bear-painted van. In a cross-cultural extravaganza, my older brother, who is a rancher, invited Tim to join him and his buddies in practicing their roping skills. Tim got acclimated by watching these real cowboys lope around the arena on their quarter horses and Morgans, twirling their lassoes and expertly catching the hind foot of a steer. Sometimes the calf outsmarted them, but it was clear that long hours of practice had brought them to the place where they could simultaneously steer a horse, twirl a rope, gauge distance and velocity, determine when to pull the lasso tight, *and* stay on the horse. After watching for a bit, the hippie from New York, who'd only ridden an old, mellow horse on a guided trail ride, mounted my brother's horse, took the reins and rope, and gave this whole cowboying skill a try. No one expected him to throw the rope in such a way that he would actually snag the calf's leg, and a few did bet he'd fall off. But he didn't, for which my brother commented, "Your rope was all over, but at least you stayed on the horse." In the cultural vernacular I grew up with, this is effusive, generous praise. This is the type of comment sons may wait decades to hear from their fathers. Such remarks are considered open-hearted in a land of sparse words, subtext, and the well-placed dirt-clump kick with your work boot to communicate the sentiments that evade you.

The message was: There is honor in finishing what you start. You don't back down, you don't chicken out, you don't change your mind. You do what you say you are going to do. Whether you want to or not, whether it works for your life now or not, whether it is what you thought it would be or not—none of those things matter. Finishing does.

The tenacity that comes with finishing strong has served me well. I've finished marathons not because I was fast or incredibly athletic but because I believed, "You can always take one more step." Tim and I served as the general contractors for our home (and had remodeled our previous home) because we believed you finish what you start. Hiring someone to do what you have skills and time to do feels like a failure. Any "owner-builder" will tell you there is a tremendous sense of pride in living in the home you built and, thinking this, I wired these lights, I laid this hardwood, I hung those cabinets. But when this mantra becomes an absolute, you lose all flexibility to dance in the moment, to stop and assess whether this next action really fulfills your mission and goals and is in accordance with your values. In a marketplace that is changing faster than ever before, leaders need to be nimble in order to see, for example, how new technology can solve a problem better or at a lower cost than the way it is currently addressed. This nimbleness depends, though, on the understanding that not all projects will get finished in the way we first imagined.

A single-minded determination to finish everything doesn't just keep us from being nimble. With that mindset, we also run the risk of becoming rigid in our self-understanding. Talking to myself with hateful words that I would never use with someone else is not going to teach me how to love other people well. Hating myself doesn't help me love others. If I tell myself I'm a loser or I can't be trusted or I'm irresponsible because I didn't finish what I started, I may very well miss the point that stopping an activity, ending a relationship, shifting the trajectory I'm on may be the braver, more authentic, and kinder choice. It may also be the harder one.

At least it was for me. Until the mid-nineties, finishing what I started had been second nature to me. All of this was to be turned on its head when Tim and I fell in love. We met at a Catholic mission in "wild, wonderful West Virginia." I quickly found out that this logo on license plates, billboards, and brochures—a slogan some ad agency had dreamed up for the state—was accurate. When I packed up my belongings, stuffed a few of them into my boyfriend's two-door hatchback car, and drove with him to Bethlehem Acres in rural West Virginia, where we had signed on to spend two years remodeling homes for low-income families, I encountered the foothills and hollers of Appalachia. They were like no place I'd known, and every day we spent driving twisty mountain roads or ripping a roof off a home built on a foundation of stacked field stone felt magical. Our work was filled with people who just did life on their own terms. There was the woman from New England who had bought a dilapidated camp across the hill and turned it into a nudist colony. There was the family down the road who made their own musical instruments *and could play them.* The butcher up the road who hunted deer . . . off his front porch . . . with a spotlight. The man who'd lived in the hollers his whole life and who claimed he could get a hawk to land on his arm.

And then there were the long-term volunteers, like me, who had signed on for a year or two to live simply in the community on $75 a month, pray together in the morning and evening, eat all our meals together—to be in solidarity with the local people and to do justice. One of our fellow volunteers had been a finance executive in New York City, left that soul-crushing rat race, moved to West Virginia, grew a beard, and gave his life a reboot climbing trees, chopping wood, and jumping in the creek. Another volunteer had been an engineer running a manufacturing plant before signing on to this mission and discerning a call to the priesthood. Another had been a contractor in Maryland and looked forward to doing some construction work that didn't require nine pages of permits. Another was about the cutest pony-tailed, muscular, guitar-playing, gregarious wood-chopping love magnet you will ever meet. When he threw his head back and laughed, the angels in heaven must have said, "Our work here is done."

Everyone had a crush on him. All the women. A few of the men. That was Tim. My future husband.

Did you catch in a previous paragraph that I went to Bethlehem Acres *with my boyfriend*?

That was Rick. Not Tim. Thus the problem and my inevitable wrestling match with "You finish what you start." It became clear to me pretty quickly, being around Rick all day long every day, that we weren't a good match. Watching his reactions to the challenges of this new environment revealed things I hadn't noticed when we were long-distance dating. You see things when you are constantly together that are different from what you see when you zip in for the weekend and fill it with visits to all the cool historic sites.

I remember getting laryngitis those first weeks at Bethlehem Acres, and I counted it a huge blessing from God that I couldn't speak, because I don't know what I would have said to Rick. Losing my voice gave me the internal time and strength to find the words I needed in order to break up with him. I realized that for a long time I had even applied a variation of "Finish what you start" to our dating relationship: "All relationships are work."

Late one night, I called home—from the *one phone* all the Bethlehem Acres volunteers shared—and was talking with my mom about this relationship. After listening to my worries, she said the wisest, most freeing words she possibly could have: "From what I've seen, the best marriages seem to be between people who laugh together a lot." Rick and I never laughed. As hard as it would be in this geographically remote location, with only seven other people on staff, I would break up with him.

In two weeks, just as soon as his parents came to visit Bethlehem Acres and drop off the rest of my stuff I had stored at their place.

Don't judge.

I had good stuff.

Once I had broken up with Rick, the dynamic changed for everyone on staff. Tim and I started spending more time together, and he was no longer available to be the life of the party. Rick was involved in his own struggle. Phil, who had liked both Tim and me, became passive-aggressive, not talking to either of us. People started openly judging Tim and me, stopping conversation when we walked into a room. I took it as the treatment I rightly deserved for hurting Rick. Breaking up was the best social capital I could have given Rick. I tried to employ my best conflict-management training, which, for me at that time, was Matthew 5:39, "Turn the other cheek." I never got mad. I never told people to stop. I never stood up for myself and said, "I acted with integrity. I didn't cheat on Rick. You have no right to judge me!" I listened, I tried to build bridges, I owned more of the situation than was mine to own.

Managing conflict using the tools I had was like trying to chop wood with a plastic knife: completely ineffective. Tim and I found ourselves out in the isolated hills of West Virginia with no car and one phone that wasn't private, living, praying, eating, and working with people who, at best, wished we hadn't fallen in love and, at the worst, hated our guts for it.

And I couldn't leave. I just couldn't. It didn't matter that there was hostility wherever I went. It didn't matter that I was developing a stutter around certain people. It didn't matter that I gained twenty pounds. (Remember, we had to eat *every meal* together, so if my mouth was stuffed, I wouldn't have to talk.) It didn't matter that this whole situation had become pathological. I couldn't leave. Because you finish what you start. You might die doing it. You might suffer every step of the way. You might be changed inextricably and forever. You might sell yourself out. But, come hell or high water, you finish what you start.

And I had sixteen months of a two-year commitment left. I could gut this out, right?

What complicated this even more for me was my understanding of how God worked. You see, this had all started when I was figuring out what to do after completing a year of service, which I had done after graduating from college. I was praying about whether God wanted me to go to Bethlehem Acres, where Rick wanted to go, or to remain as an alternate for an international music ministry I really wanted to be part of, which would mean Rick and I would be continents apart. I had been praying for several weeks about this, and one day, out of the blue, I felt a voice say, "Get a Bible—your answer is in the Bible." So I quickly found a Bible and thought, "If I open to anything that talks about building, I'll know I'm supposed to go to West Virginia." I opened to Ezra 4:13—about rebuilding the temple in Jerusalem. Easy enough—God had spoken. So I got ready. I bought sturdy Redwing work boots at a discounted price in the kid section (the gift of small feet). I found a pair of overalls at Goodwill. I packed my belongings, and away Rick and I went.

God had brought me to West Virginia for a two-year stay. I *knew* this in the depths of my being, and if God had brought me to West Virginia, God needed to give me the word that it was okay to leave. So I did what I had done while discerning whether to come here: I prayed for an answer. Beside the creek that ran behind our house and the greenhouse in our little holler, I prayed and prayed.

And nothing came.

I learned later that during this same time, my mom and middle brother were so worried that they considered coming and picking me up—doing an intervention of sorts. They could hear over the phone how distressed I was. Also, Tim was implementing an exit strategy. His theological understanding was that God gives you common sense, and if your common sense tells you it is time to go, get the hell outta there! He didn't buy into the lie that you've gotta finish what you start.

Tim was planning to leave, but he was determined not to go without me. He knew I would be eaten alive if I stayed alone. So, on a Saturday at the end of April, we loaded my stuff—I had good stuff—into Tim's family's van that his brother had driven down from New York. After listening patiently to me for hours over the course of several weeks as I tried to figure out what to do and whether I would be letting God down, that morning Tim literally took my hand and said, "It's time to go."

It was eight months since I had arrived—sixteen months short of what I had committed to. I didn't know what I'd do next. I hadn't finished. Heck, some might say I had barely started.

Finding My Way to Truth: Moderation

Maybe you can relate to my story more than you wish. Maybe you are in a ministry or leadership position that isn't life-giving, where there is conflict and you feel stuck, where you feel ineffective or that your talents and gifts aren't going to ever be seen in this place. Thoughts like "Well, this is as good as it is going to get" might lurk on the edges of your mind, keeping you wedged up against indecision. This lie pretends to be so noble because, well, don't we all want to finish strong? In ministry and leadership don't we all want to run the race set before us? But how do we know if the race set before us is a sprint, mid-distance, or a marathon if we haven't stopped to discern instead of just blindly believing this lie? When a pastor or deacon discerns with intention about when and how to leave a call, the transition is healthier. When we pay attention, reflect, and then apply to our decisions what we have learned, those decisions become more authentic, more real to us.

Pay Attention

In my Bethlehem Acres situation, it was easy to see the clues that this lie was sucking the life out of me. I gained weight. I was anxious, filled with self-doubt most of the time. I lived in chronic stress for five months and actually was beginning to develop a stutter. I was losing my ability to trust myself and my decisions. I felt unmoored, directionless, and lost. In addition to fear, I felt shame, anger, and despair. People around me—my mom, my brother, and Tim— knew my mental health was suffering.

Examine

In this particular situation, the lie that you must finish what you start felt to me like a point of redemption—that if I stuck it out, I would redeem myself from the hurt Tim's and my decision to date had caused other people. It would prove that I was emotionally strong, like a fourteenth-century monk or a twentieth-century missionary to a foreign land: long-suffering but dutifully faithful. Upon reflection, I realize I didn't have any positive examples of people stopping before they had finished a commitment. So if I quit, I wondered, what would people think? What would my parents think? What would my high school classmates think? I was thinking far too much about what other people might think of me! Leaving felt like a failure, like Tim and I were wrong to be dating, like I wouldn't be able to hold my head high. Like there was some emotional prize for sticking it out, and the prize was exoneration.

I also naïvely believed that I could love people into being a healthy community. That wasn't going to work. It is not the responsibility of the abused to take care of the abuser. I let people treat me poorly; Tim didn't. He didn't have the hang-ups about conflict I did. When Phil, one of our fellow volunteers, had declared to Tim in the tool shed that he didn't think it was right that Tim and I were dating, if it had been me amid the rakes and crosscut saws, I would have listened and repeated back his concerns so he knew I'd heard him. Tim was not about such metered, diplomatic robo-language. He was about flexing his muscular forearms and saying, "The only one who can judge Sarah and me is God, and you are not God."

I didn't have boundaries, so leaving—the ultimate boundary—seemed unfathomable to me. In the months that followed our departure from Bethlehem Acres, I struggled much more mightily with deep, abiding anger than Tim did. I think because he had stood up for himself and me, he could move on more easily. I wrestled with all the things I wished I had said but never did. I fantasized about writing a whole batch of cruel, hate-filled—anonymous—letters to those with whom, just months before, I'd sat in a prayer circle. I allowed vindictiveness to fill my heart for too long. I never did these things, but they sure kept me company as I tried to figure out how to move forward.

When I dig into this lie, the irony isn't lost on me that Tim and I have been married for twenty years, that we've been together for twenty-five years. We *are* finishing what we started. If I switch my thinking and expand on it, yes, Bethlehem Acres was what brought us together, but what I needed to continue wasn't my commitment to the Acres but to Tim. The piece of the story I haven't yet shared is that Tim had a sense when he graduated from college that he was meant to go to Bethlehem Acres because he was "supposed to" meet someone there. Several of his college friends were going to Utah to volunteer with another program and, in their free time, to ski the slopes. They pressed hard for Tim to go with them, but he felt drawn to return to West Virginia, where he had volunteered several times during college, because he was "supposed to" meet someone there. Me. The first weekend our staff was all at Bethlehem Acres, when I'd been there only three days, we all went out dancing. Tim had a friend, Colleen, visiting from college. Everyone was dancing with everyone, different couples for each song. When Tim and I finished dancing, Colleen said to him, "You are going to marry that girl." Five years later when he did, Colleen baked the Communion bread for our wedding. I believe in the depths of my heart that God brought us together, but when and how we left Bethlehem Acres God left up to us.

Apply the Learning

There is a difference between tenacity and unexamined worship of the lie about finishing what one has started. Tenacity means I will work really hard, stick with something even when it is uncomfortable, even if I won't see the fruits of my efforts for months or even years. An example from my life is marketing my work as a "solopreneur" facilitator and speaker. I've planted seeds that haven't taken root for years, but then out of the blue they do, and a new opportunity emerges. Tenacity isn't soul-crushing; it doesn't ask me to sell myself out. It asks me to be *more* of myself.

Second, I've also come to appreciate the gift of exhaustion. For years, I had just pushed through, borrowing the needed time from sleep. I know I'm not alone in there being vast stretches of years when I was exhausted and didn't do anything about it. After our second child, Jacob, was born, Tim and I developed a new habit—drinking coffee—but even with two pots a day, I found myself jealous of residents living in long-term care. I'd see someone taking a nap in the afternoon and think, "You don't know how good you have it! You get to sleep whenever you want, and someone else does your laundry and cooks for you." You know you're losing your grip on reality when you are envious of someone who needs full-time care.

Now when I get tired, instead of denying it and trying to hide it, I see the potential blessing in it: the permission to slow down, to leave some things for tomorrow, and to leave some things for someone else to bring into the world. To switch course takes courage because you might not know what is coming down the tracks next. But I've learned that putting the brakes on the "finish-it" bullet train means I am trusting God more to lead me and trusting my gut more to help me set limits—and that if a project feels like a mismatch, I can listen to that intuition.

I now enjoy having "white space" in my schedule and not feeling the constant need to do the next thing on the list because I've got to get it all done. I've learned to ask myself questions such as, "Does it really matter? Will this bring our family joy? Is this soul-food for me?"

Life is kinder this way. *I* am kinder this way.

Finally, I've learned that when you are in a deep, dark place like I was at Bethlehem Acres, you need help. You need someone who can help you see the light and get out of your destructive thinking. Then, you can integrate that learning with your other life experiences so you will be stronger moving forward and will have more to offer those around you.

Honestly, as a parent I sometimes worry that I'm not instilling a solid work ethic into our kids if I let them drop out of something. I can quickly convince myself that when things get hard in life, they will buckle under the pressure. But in the end, the stronger lesson—stronger than making them finish the Halloween costume they started or the fort they began to build—is what Tim and I do teach them: to finish what they start but not to the point that they kill themselves doing it. If they realize they are headed to a wrong destination, it is okay to jump off the "finish-it" bullet train. It is okay to try something and learn that it isn't your thing. No shame in that.

If you walked into our house at suppertime, you'd notice that after we'd prayed "Come, Lord Jesus" or another prayer, we'd talk about school and the day's events, and we just might talk about how it is good to have boundaries and to check in with yourself and what your gut may be telling you. You might hear us tell our kids to surround themselves with people who treat them well—and to treat themselves well.

And, as we clear our dishes, you just might notice some rogue peas and pizza crusts left on our plates.

4.

"I Must Follow the Rules"

Discernment

I am a rule follower, and it bugs me when other people break the rules. For example, at the Sistine Chapel, I missed much of the beauty of the fresco ceiling and the painting of Adam reaching for God because I just wanted to tell all the other tourists to be quiet. I was annoyed because people weren't following the instruction to be quiet. This isn't just *my* issue—this is *an* issue. It is an issue of such magnitude that there are official shushers in the chapel. There are literally guards in the Sistine Chapel who hush and shush people all day. See, we wouldn't have to have shusher-guards if we all could just follow the rule posted by the entrance, to be respectfully silent. We can follow the rule for fifteen minutes, right? We can do this, people!

Or showering only once a week. I did that for eight months because that was the rule at the little Catholic mission in the foothills of West Virginia where I met my husband, Tim. The logic behind the rule was that because the county we were in was, at the time, the poorest county in the poorest state of the United States, we should be in solidarity with the local people, some of whom had no running water at all. Well, Tim broke the rule because he believed it was just a cover-up for an undersized septic system. This caused something of a moral crisis for me. I had to think long and hard about whether I could date a rule breaker. Eventually I realized we were like two magnets being drawn together and nothing was going to prevent this attraction—not even the showering situation or Tim's flagrant disregard for the rules. Try falling in love when you do construction work all day in the heat and shower *very* infrequently. That is true love!

But that wasn't the only place where Tim's rule-breaking was an issue for me. You see, I wasn't sure I could be with someone who swore, and he did occasionally use colorful language, and he did more than once take the name of the Lord in vain—both of which he may have said when I brought up my concern about his language. He then wondered if *he* could be with someone who was so judgmental. We worked our way through what was adiaphora (*adiaphora* is my favorite among the "big words" I carry with me from seminary; it means "secondary things not core to the main purpose or the main action"), and what was authentic for each of us and worked for us both. We settled on restraint from using the Lord's name in vain, but the rest was all good. The irony is that a few years later, I was the potty mouth and he was the one raising an eyebrow. When our son was a toddler and started muttering "damn it" under his breath, we all knew who had had the parent fail. Me. I guess I'm a rule follower until a messy house and sleep deprivation catch up with me.

I want there to be a good reason for breaking a rule, not just a willy-nilly reason intended to cause harm or disruption—or to dispel frustration. National Day of Silence is April 11, a day when people who are LGBTQIA+ and their allies in school are silent; they don't answer questions in class or talk. That is breaking the rule "Answer when you are called on" in order to build awareness about how the voices of people who are

LGBTQIA+ are silenced daily. That is rule-breaking with a good reason. But some rules don't make a lot of sense. Or the reason for the rule no longer applies, or doesn't apply as broadly as the rule is typically presented. And who gets to make the rules? What is the purpose of the rule? What rules do I make up for myself that I perpetually break because I'm only half-heartedly committed to them? I can readily name several: getting eight hours of sleep, exercising daily, no dessert. What rules do we believe are sacrosanct, but if we questioned them, we would see they are kinda willy-nilly? Not all rules are created equal.

The church throughout time has been really good at some of these willy-nilly rules. I'm not talking about the guards sternly saying, "Silencio!" every three minutes under Michelangelo's masterpiece. They absolutely need to be there. I'm talking about rules that aren't life-giving, that do more damage than good, that make broken people who seek healing *more* broken. Rules that have wounded people I've loved and served.

Let me tell you about Gertrude. She was self-contained, not given to effusive conversation, or to even much engagement with other residents at the long-term care center where she had lived for almost two years. She sat quietly in worship as I presided, but she never received Holy Communion. Twenty years ago, being a young woman in ministry among people in their seventies and eighties, I was well aware that for many of them, my very person broke the rules for what a pastor *should* be and how a pastor *should* look. I wondered if the reason Gertrude never received Holy Communion was that she didn't believe women should be ordained. I knew I didn't look like the icon of a pastor for people who were confirmed in the 1920s; I looked more like their granddaughter or great-niece. While passing out hymnals one day before Bible study, I overheard a resident say to her neighbor, "That skirt is so tight, I don't know how she sits down." As people age, some lose their social filter, and when their friends are hard of hearing, you overhear things about you that were never intended for you to hear. Or at least I hope I wasn't intended to hear that! Yes, my skirt was a bit snug but no snugger than what other women my age wore. I didn't pop the buttons off as I sat down to open my Bible to Matthew's Gospel, and the skirt was a modest mid-calf length. But a pastor who was not only a woman but a woman who sometimes wore tight skirts—scandalous! It seemed I was breaking one of those willy-nilly, nebulous rules about what modesty looks like.

Let me tell you about the notebook I found while cleaning up after worship one day. A man's name was written in the upper right-hand corner of the first page, and on all of the subsequent pages were notes about the worship services—not confirmation sermon notes, which require the writer to reflect on how the Gospel lesson and sermon tied together, where they heard law and where they heard gospel, how they will live out that teaching, and so forth. No, these were pages of notes on how the service was organized. Start and end times were recorded, along with commentary—sermon was too long, sermon was too short, second hymn played too quickly. While looking at this record, it struck me that the adiaphora were recorded; the secondary things were listed. What was he missing in worship if the point of coming to worship was to critique details? If you have a need to critique the deets, you could do that while getting your tires changed—rotation was 6:23 on right front tire, on rear left it was 5:38. Willy-nilly!

And then there was the guy who attended worship, sat in the back, and one day before worship asked me what the first word of the Lord's Prayer was. It definitely felt like some kind of a test, and he was the one giving it, and I was the one who needed to pass. "Our," I said—I know the Lord's Prayer, thank you very much, have known it for years. And he said, "Our. It is Ou-ur. Not *are*." Does that really matter? Never mind different dialects! Adiaphora. If you ever attend worship when I'm leading and you hear me over-enunciate "ou-ur" like I'm doing warm-up exercises before a limerick competition, you can thank Lloyd for that. Willy-nilly all the way.

Gertrude wasn't the one who had commented on my skirt, or tracked my sermon length, or corrected my open vowels. But this type of microscopic focus was on my mind when Gertrude asked me to visit her privately. I went with some trepidation, wondering how to graciously receive a tongue-lashing if my assumption was correct and this was about women in ministry.

Her room was warmly decorated—clean, tidy, the Hummels and teacups mindfully arranged—not too many, but just the right number to remind her of home and still keep the dusting manageable. She got right to the point: "I suppose you are wondering why I don't receive Communion." What followed was a story that broke my heart. A story, sadly, that I had heard other elders tell with details of their own lives. A story that had nothing to do with me as a woman in ministry but had everything to do with adiaphora, with rules that were death-dealing. Rules that were willy-nilly, with no real reason to be that way.

Like so many of her generation, Gertrude had a childhood filled with loss, instability, responsibilities well beyond her age, and few protections. She told me that her mother had died when she was just eleven or twelve. Her mother's death was heartbreaking, of course, but it also meant that Gertrude now assumed the role of helping to raise her younger siblings. When the time came for confirmation instruction, she attended with her classmates, quickly assuming care of the household upon returning home. When Confirmation Day finally came, when students would receive Holy Communion for the first time, although Gertrude had taken all the classes, the pastor wouldn't allow her to be confirmed because her father couldn't afford to buy the white dress girls were required to wear for the occasion.

Let me repeat that: because she was too poor to have the right clothes, she wasn't confirmed.

A cascade of questions flooded my mind. Oh, Lord, how can we get it so wrong? Why didn't her father fight the injustice of classism and shaming? (He probably had no energy and maybe even believed the stigma that had been placed upon them.) If others in the church knew this was a rule, why didn't some kind soul anonymously buy her the required white dress? If no one else could afford to buy the dress for her, why didn't someone loan her one? Because if this rule was adhered to for every Confirmation Sunday, there must have been white dresses hanging in closets all across the county. Why hadn't the pastor been helpful? When he learned she didn't have the white dress, why didn't he find one? Why was no one looking out for her? Why didn't he see the damage he was about to do? Why did he love a rule more than a person? Why did she matter less than the order of things?

A white dress intended to represent the righteousness found in Christ became a lifelong symbol of deepest shame and worthlessness.

That pastor was following the rules; he was doing what was expected of him. Maybe he had a *Little House on the Prairie* Harriet Oleson type in his congregation who would berate him on Monday morning if he had broken with tradition at the Sunday Confirmation. I don't know why he did what he did, but I do have a sense of the lifelong consequence of the choices that were made seventy years before. Gertrude was in her eighties when she bravely shared this story. She'd gone to church—off and on—her *whole* life, she had been married in the church, she'd had her children baptized and confirmed, and she never . . . received . . . Holy . . . Communion.

How quickly *holy* moved from making whole hearts to making holes in hearts. Adiaphora.

Maybe because I was a woman in ministry and looked nothing like what pastors were "supposed to" look like; maybe because my skirt was a little tight and I didn't have a bellowing preacher voice and I cried occasionally while preaching; maybe because I was breaking the rules of what a pastor *should* be, she finally felt she had permission to share her story. Maybe because I looked nothing like the pastor of her youth, she felt safe to be real and authentic with me. Maybe all the things about me that others had viewed as points of suspicious concern were, for her, invitations. Or maybe it had very little to do with me. Maybe after years, after decades of going to church and feeling less-than and unworthy, watching others process up to the altar rail and kneel, you just get tired of believing a lie someone told you years ago about who you are, and you simply have had enough. Maybe instead of having enough, it is time to recognize, *I am enough.*

Rules were followed, and a life—instead of bread for her—was broken. The very thing Jesus gave us as a reminder of God's love was, for her, a reminder of being an outsider, not brought closer to God but pushed further away. How many confirmation services did she sit through across those decades? Of how much joy, peace, and self-love had following the rules robbed Gertrude?

As I sat on Gertrude's damask loveseat, I didn't hear

anger in her voice. I heard the need to be understood. She wanted me to know why she didn't receive Holy Communion, that was all. She didn't want me to fix it, change it, or right the wrongs of the past, even though I tried. I told her she was a beloved child of God and she could receive Holy Communion right that very moment if she wanted, and I asked, how could I best love her in this moment? No, that wasn't what she wanted, not in that conversation anyway. She just wanted to be heard and understood. So instead of forcing something that didn't come from her, I let it be. This was her story and her timeline. She got to decide what happened next and when it happened. We agreed I would visit again soon.

But before soon came, her death did—about two weeks later.

Why didn't I return sooner? Why didn't I push harder? That is a regret for me. I want to tell you a story that says when I returned, we studied her denomination's catechism, and she reaffirmed her baptism—that with a beautiful ending, her life was brought full circle. I want the story to end with her receiving Holy Communion with the congregation in our little makeshift care center chapel, with her smiling and feeling fully loved by God for the first time in her life. Her daughter might even have snapped a picture of her and her grandson after worship before the daughter would whisper to me conspiratorially and with a light squeeze on my arm, "This means more than you know!"

But not all stories follow the rule that if you've suffered, you deserve and get a happy ending, or at least the ending we'd like to write. I had to explain this to our ten-year-old son when he asked why one of his favorite authors, five books into a series, killed off the main character. Not all stories end the way we would write them. I don't want the story to end with death snatching away from Gertrude the healing of the shame and sadness a church leader had rained on her.

Yet the fact that she didn't receive Holy Communion doesn't inherently mean Gertrude didn't experience healing and peace. That is the story my fear is making up. All of our stories are unique, and maybe she received what she needed or wanted to receive. After all, she didn't ask me to hurry up and see her again when I greeted her in the dining room or the next time we were together in worship. I simply know that, as her chaplain, *I* wanted the story to end differently. In my estimation, the pastor of her youth let her down, and I'm aware that to some degree, the same assessment could be made of my ministry; I could have done more. My regret is one known to anyone who has ever cared for or loved someone who died. It is a regret that comes easily for any of us in positions of responsibility for the health and welfare of others: there is always more we could have done, if we had only known.

It is easy to say in some self-righteous judgment, "Well, we are better now. The church has learned; we've moved on. Look at what people wear to church these days!" And we have learned. You go to church with me, and you can wear whatever you want on whatever Sunday it is. But some churches still practice shunning. I've counseled people who have had that experience. While they do not officially condone shunning, some congregations have such a long and strong culture of conformity upheld by judgment and shaming that it isn't a safe place to share, for example, that you recently got divorced. How in the world do we believe that these types of actions are going to speak of God's love in a broken world? In my estimation this isn't about grace; this is intended to bellow a public service announcement about what good Christians do and don't do. According to this thinking, good Christians get a white dress and good Christians don't mess up and good Christians don't get divorced, and if you don't fit into the category of good Christian, then here's your T-shirt that says, "My purpose in life is to be the bad example your mother warned you about."

What do we love more? The simplicity of always keeping the rules even when doing so destroys life? Or loving people even when it makes keeping the rules messy? I believe that rules, at their best, serve people by providing safety, structure, opportunity to learn and grow, and social cohesion.

The problem with following the rules all the time is that we can miss the very people we are called to serve and lead. Our actions can come from a misinformed place. Much as Jesus switched the understanding of the meaning of Sabbath—"The sabbath was made for humankind, and not humankind for the sabbath" (Mark 2:27)—we have to ask: Do the rules serve the people? Or do the *people* serve the rules?

When you are trying to lead well, how do you decide what rules to follow and what to let slide? Do you let it slide because that is the course of least resistance or because overlooking the rule might be the most loving thing to do? For me, this dilemma quickly moved from theoretical to practical one spring day when my phone rang. There are calls you are not prepared to answer, because you haven't ever had to respond to that type of situation before. Because the situation is uncommon enough that you never thought about it or you never heard your peers wondering about it. While companies, hospitals, care centers, and clinics have disaster response protocols, when you are a parish pastor, the response doesn't usually—if ever—follow an organizational chart, or even the practices taught in pastoral care classes in seminary. The response follows what the moment needs, for there to be the greatest sense of God's love and presence.

The church secretary was calling, saying she had just gotten off the phone with a man who said he knew me. He asked if I could quickly come to the hospital and baptize their baby because their baby had died during delivery.

It was one of the hardest calls I've ever answered.

As I quickly drove to the hospital, I knew the theological quandary I was in: to break the doctrinal rule and baptize their deceased child, or follow the rule that baptism is for the living and break the parents' hearts even further than they were already broken? Following doctrinal rules is a big deal for pastors. A seminarian who is seeking ordination in a specific denomination knows that their personal life, beliefs, and theology will all be evaluated. For four years. For example, my internship supervisor had to check a box confirming that I consistently wore my seat belt. Check. Your theology is reviewed, and if your theology doesn't conform to the denomination's doctrinal positions, you may be denied endorsement to become a pastor. And once ordained, you can always be defrocked. Some pastors, as they grow throughout their careers and as their denomination changes, eventually experience dissonance to such a level that they switch denominations because the institution's theology and the pastor's theology no long resonate with each other. So, choosing to baptize an infant who had died wasn't a small decision; it potentially carried large consequences for me.

I called a mentor pastor, who didn't tell me what to do but gave me a lot of grace to meet the family where they were emotionally and promised she would be praying for me. I also knew the pastoral care ethic I held: you respect and honor the values and beliefs of those you serve while also respecting and honoring your own values and beliefs. This meant, for example, while I would absolutely pray with a Catholic resident who was dying, I won't give that same resident Last Rites because I'm not a priest. It would be disingenuous for me to present myself as something I wasn't.

I knew my denomination's understanding, the rule, about baptism. Baptism is for the living. You don't baptize the dead, because this isn't magic water. I'd never witnessed a baptism of someone who was deceased, nor did my pastoral colleagues even talk about these situations. I also knew that how those of us who represent the church and God show up matters deeply. What we say, how we say it, what boundaries we hold all matter and will be remembered long after a moment has passed. In these critical moments people are looking for something holy to hold on to. I didn't know the particulars of this couple's beliefs. I did know that in their darkest hour, they called the church, and in my opinion, the church had better show up for them.

When I arrived at the hospital, the nurse assigned to this couple was waiting for me. I told her I'd never been in this situation before, and she discreetly told me that often pastors would say a prayer. She was doing her best to support me. "But the call I got said they wanted the baby to be baptized," I said. Then without a word of disapproval, she showed me the sacramental supplies the hospital kept on hand for baptisms in an emergency, when the child may not survive. Some small shells, a few small cloths, and a vial of oil.

When I walked into the hospital room, the mom was holding their child, who was bundled, as many newborns are, in a flannel blanket. The baby's dad behind her, an arm wrapped around her and their baby, as if trying to shield them both from some further anticipated danger. They placed their baby into my arms, wearing the hospital-standard pastel pink-and-blue hat my children would wear years later.

It is one of the rawest moments of my ministry. I had been with many people as they died and with their families afterward, but mostly these were elders who had prayed at one time or another that God would take them home. These were people who had been on hospice for months, and their families had had time to say goodbye. Those deaths were still hard—an earthly life ended—but they followed the natural order of things. This was entirely different.

In a voice barely audible and through tears that fell on the infant I held, I said, "Child of God, I baptize you in the name of the Father, the Son, and the Holy Spirit."

I broke the rule.

Maybe a different pastor could have explained the theological tension in a life-giving way and redirected the parents away from baptism to ensure that the church's response didn't add to the heartbreak of this tragedy. Maybe a different pastor who had known them for years, been in adult Bible studies with them, placed the body of Christ in their hands in worship, and knew their hearts could have gently and tenderly denied the request and still held their pain. Maybe a different pastor could have quickly put together a ritual that provided the reassurance of God's love for their child without using water and a cloth. But those pastors weren't the one called.

I was. They chose to call me. It turned out that I knew them casually through a friend of a friend from a running club. Our relationship wasn't a traditional pastor-parishioner relationship; their picture wasn't in our church directory. I didn't even know I was considered "their" pastor. Until I received the call.

Finding My Way to Truth: Discernment

Just as rules can exist willy-nilly—without our understanding why—rule-breaking can also be willy-nilly—when we aren't clear why breaking the rule is our most authentic action. The gift God gave to me on my drive to the hospital was discernment.

Pay Attention

What was my body telling me on the drive to the birthing center? I freaked out a bit before getting in the car, but as I drove, my breath became steady and my mind peacefully emptied. I developed laser focus. Underneath my sadness and uncertainty about how to do this was an abiding sense of call and calm: call—that God was bringing me to be with this family; and calm—that I could trust my gut on what was pastoral. By being aware of my body, thoughts, and emotions, I knew that I had strength.

Examine

My regret about not doing enough for Gertrude motivated my decision in the hospital. I don't regret what I did for the family, because I firmly believe that if I had not baptized their child, they would have wondered if the church—as loosely as they were connected to it—and God had turned away from them in their darkest hour—or shown up at only a comfortable distance. For me personally, I don't believe God was disappointed in my choice. I am not usually a renegade, and in fact, as I revealed at the beginning of this chapter, I readily endorse following the rules, even if they don't make a lot of sense. But here was a stunned, grieving couple who could do one thing, *one thing*, for their child: have their beloved baptized. There was no way I would add to their pain. Their story wasn't going to include church-induced trauma. Given the factors I had in front of me that day, breaking a doctrinal rule looked like the most loving route to take.

Apply the Learning

Let me be clear: I'm not talking about breaking safety rules, like practicing proper medication stewardship or reporting work comp injuries or following the Individualized Education Plan. I'm not talking about wantonly hurting others or putting them in danger because we don't want to follow a rule. I'm talking about breaking rules that aren't going to serve those we serve.

In leadership, we will be confronted with ethical situations for which we didn't receive specific training. Given a thousand other factors, I may have made a different choice—if I were older, if I had more of a relationship with this family, if they were members of my congregation, if the circumstances around their baby's death hadn't been so traumatic. The key is to know *how* you make decisions. What will your litmus test be? Initially, I didn't share this story with many colleagues because I feared their judgment. I feared I would be told how wrong my decision was and that I shouldn't have done what I did. But over the years, the more I've brought this story out of the shadows and have shared it, the more other leaders have told their stories of breaking established rules. And our reasoning is fairly similar: breaking the rule was the most life-giving option.

Even though the official shusher-guards do good, important work in the Sistine Chapel, sometimes we do need to break the rules and speak up, because the words we speak are what fill the gap between the hand of God and the hand of a wounded person reaching for healing.

5.

"I Have to Be Nice"

Boundaries

If you are a certain age, I bet you can fill in the blanks:
"If you can't say something nice, don't _____
_____ ____ _____."[1] In the Disney classic
Bambi, Thumper's mother gives this sage advice over and
over. Many of us were raised on the axiom. The heart of
this is true and helpful: be mindful of your words, know
what you are saying and why, don't malign another's
character, put the best possible construction on another's
actions, be polite and respectful. In a culture and time when
cynicism and personal attack seem to be not just tolerated
but at times encouraged and rewarded, I'm all for these
behaviors.

I'm not alone in putting a premium on niceness. Here
in Minnesota, where I live, we have gained a national
reputation for "being nice." It even has a name: Minnesota
Nice. After the 2018 Super Bowl was held in the "Bold
North," we sighed in relief that visitors, for the most part,
found us agreeable, even though the weather was far too
cold for some guests. People who move to Minnesota from
other parts of the country or world notice immediately that

---

1. Just in case you're not of that certain age or the person who raised you
   happened not to use this proverb, here are the four words: "say anything at
   all."

we are polite, helpful, and, well, nice—not in a Southern, hug-n-love kinda way but in our reserved, modest manner.

Underneath the civility and our offers to help, however, you will find the soft underbelly of Minnesota Nice: passive-aggressive behavior. Minnesota Nice, meet Minnesota Nasty. We avoid speaking the uncomfortable truth . . . that may *need* to be spoken. We avoid certain topics or don't hold someone accountable for their destructive or inappropriate behavior, accepting or excusing it with "Oh, well, that's just Aunt Beth." Or "That's just how he is." We may be quiet, but that doesn't ensure agreement on a topic. Ask your Minnesota Nice boss if you can take Friday afternoon off, and then it so happens that your kid is sick the next Monday and you can't come to work. When you do return to work, that boss might slip into Minnesota Nasty with a little passive-aggressive zinger: "Well, I haven't seen *you* in a while!"

Or if you delay returning a phone call because you have to share some hard news for which you will probably be judged, you've just been Minnesota Nastied if, when you do call, the other person answers the phone by saying, "I can't believe I'm actually talking to you! I was about ready to file a missing-person report!"

Or if you forget to proof an important document and your coworker saves your butt by catching spelling errors, that coworker just might be on the shadow side of Minnesota Nice if, the next five times you are turning in an important document, they say, "Have you spell-checked it? Or do you need some help with that again?"

A little *LEGO® Movie* reference can give us a visual. In this animation, all the characters are LEGO® figures. One police officer is both the Good Cop and the Bad Cop. One moment cheerful Good Cop is nice and helpful with a chirpy smile, and the next moment, his yellow head spins

180 degrees, and Bad Cop is now on the job with his snide comments, gravelly voice, and menacing grimace. Minnesota Nice becomes Minnesota Nasty just as quickly when it starts subtly picking at someone's imperfections. And if someone takes offense, Minnesota Nasty, not wanting to be caught, might say, "Oh gosh, I was just joking! I didn't know you were so sensitive."

I'm being Minnesota Nice with my family when I cook, set the table, clear the table, do the dishes, and huff and puff the whole time. I know I'm *really* sucked into resentment when my spouse offers to help and I say, "No, I got it." On the surface that could look, well, nice. I'm letting him relax while I do the work. But really, I'm rejecting his help because now I'm feeling righteously wronged, and that feels more comfortable than letting some of my anger go and getting help with the crusted-over casserole pan.

Some of us in the Land of 10,000 Lakes feel that our signature way of being is undeservedly under assault and have taken to wearing T-shirts campaigning to "Keep Minnesota passive-aggressive." I knew this movement was gaining popularity when I saw a friend wearing a shirt with the "Keep Minnesota passive-aggressive" phrase in bold letters and underneath, in a smaller font, the words "Or you decide. Whatever you think is best." I laughed out loud when I read that because it is so true! These T-shirts have far less to do with promoting respect than with passive-aggressively calling out passive-aggressive behavior.

Passive-aggressive behavior is more destructive than many of us are ready to admit. While we may tell ourselves that the silent treatment is better than saying something cruel, we are creating environments where people always have to be on guard. Some Midwestern stoics seem to believe we receive a finite allotment of words in our lifetime, so we'd best use them wisely. If slamming a pot down can communicate our irritation or anger, we can conserve our words. While putting up pickles, our mothers and grandmothers taught us to stir the pot while never uttering a sound. And while walking beans, our grandfathers and fathers made us shape up with a well-placed withering look.

Making someone else guess what the silent treatment means is a manipulative way to wield power. It is a subversive form of power-over. Every time we say "I'm *fine!*" through gritted teeth and with a heavy sigh, we tell those around us that we are anything *but* fine and that, therefore, *they* are not fine. And, sadly, it tells them we are pretty fine with things remaining as they are. Not because the status quo is life-giving, but rather because we aren't able, equipped, or ready to move forward, to own our part, to name someone else's behavior that we find destructive to our well-being. Some of us honestly don't know other ways of communicating.

Of course, there are too many situations to name in which challenging someone, naming a dynamic that needs to change, can lead to some form of harm or danger to ourselves or others. When we have named something that has so much power in a relationship or group, even naming it can cause others to attack the truth-teller. When we are in such toxic environments, being passive becomes a form of survival, and professional help is needed to move the relationship or group forward—or to help us exit that relational space to safety.

In situations where physical, emotional, or verbal abuse isn't part of the dynamic, however, passive-aggressive actions send the message that whatever is between us is too big, too much for us to handle—much less resolve or move through. Passive-aggressive behavior drives the lie that we might as well settle for what we have, because things could always be worse. Enduring a known problem feels safer than stepping into new territory.

Whether the "nice" we attempt to practice is truly nice or merely passive-aggressive, it can be harmful when it drives us away from each other, when it lies to us and says, "Snippy, well-placed zingers are your best option." It lies to us and says we aren't strong enough to weather real hurts and challenges in relationships. It then does a bait-n-switch, telling us that peace obtained at any cost is truly peaceful and that if we just pray hard enough or turn the other cheek enough times or bear one another's burdens long enough, things will change. But things don't change. So Nice, like the frenemy who connivingly spins frenzied drama, sits beside us, rubs our shoulder, and says, "On the bright side, if you keep pretending, at least you *look* like everything is fine." Like if we can't have real, genuine connection with others, the consolation prize is a shellacked façade of what we think real connection would be. So we show up at church, or an extended-family event, or a community gathering, just barely holding it together, dying on the inside but pretending all is well and thinking that "Fake it 'til you make it" can apply not just to overcoming fear of public speaking but to healing hearts too. And as we make small-chat over donuts and coffee, or while watching the kids splash in the lake, or while cheering for the hometown volleyball team, we might concede, "Yeah, I suppose Nice is right. At least other people think I'm fine. I guess that counts for something."

And then Nice, with a pat on our knee, gets up, pauses before walking away, and drops, "Or, you know, whatever you think is best. Your choice."

I imagine you can see by now, I am well versed in Nice. But I, for one, am done with it.

I want to live with *Kind.* I want to be kind. For me this

means I live with integrity; I care about my words and how they impact people; I choose to say what needs to be said without attacking, demeaning, discounting others, or poking at their vulnerabilities. To paraphrase Martin Luther's interpretation of the eighth commandment, as much as it depends on me, I want to speak well of my neighbor and come to my neighbor's defense. And I want you to be kind. I want to surround myself with kind people. People who say in word and deed, "When you fall, I will help you get to your feet. I've got some bandages right here, and you can have them." People who will offer a soft place to land in a world filled with hard edges. People who say, "I love you no matter what." Kind-hearted people.

Kind hasn't been co-opted and corrupted like Nice has. The T-shirts I see promoting kindness simply encourage me to "Be kind" or "Choose kind." There are no footnotes. Kind includes all the positive, life-giving qualities of Nice while leaving behind the T-shirt–inspiring baggage.

This switch from Nice to Kind can seem like simply an exercise in wordsmithing. "Oh, great, now I can never say, 'It was so nice that you put the toilet seat down.'" Or because I read this book, now I'm supposed to say to a new acquittance, "Kind to meet you." Or I've got to monitor myself, so I expunge my vocabulary of "nice." I'm not talking about changing what word we use. I'm talking about *understanding our actions better* so we are empowered to live more authentic lives and have more rewarding, more honest relationships with the people we love and work with.

Even if we are ready to admit that passive-aggressive actions are soul-sucking and that distancing behavior masquerading as nice (if you can't say anything nice, don't say anything at all—just huff and puff around the house) isn't mature, we may have little sense of what to replace them with. Or even the sense that we *get* to. That we *get* to acknowledge frustration in relationships, and we *get* to work for something better. But here is the thing: we *get* to do that! Changing relationship patterns takes courage to start, and it takes practice to continue. It is hard work, and you'll take a thousand steps backward as you move forward. But the sense of grounded authenticity you'll gain is so worth the effort. You will get your self back by feeling stronger and more energized, and in doing so, you will have richer, deeper, more honest relationships with the people you love.

Finding My Way to Truth: Boundaries

If we want to change our own behavior from being nice to being kind, the place to begin is with boundaries. Boundaries are everywhere. A boundary is the property line that marks for everyone where one person's property ends and someone else's property begins. Boundaries—in schools, work environments, churches, public transit—delineate what you can do in a certain space and what you can't. Boundaries are good and healthy when they keep people safe and productive. Emotional boundaries have the same intent: to keep us safe and living in right relationships with other people. Emotional boundaries are connected to how I allow people to talk to me, how I talk with other people, what I will or won't feel responsible for, whether I am helping someone or enabling bad habits. Kindness and boundaries are really good friends. Kindness means we help others know how to treat us, because we risk being honest and authentic with them about what works for us, what doesn't, what needs to change, how the change can work. We don't expect others to read our minds, which is fairly passive (and can even be aggressive).

Pay Attention

Setting and maintaining life-giving boundaries isn't a once-and-done deal. It is a lifelong task that begins with self-awareness—knowing what is going on in our emotions, thoughts, and behaviors.

Physically: When an emotional boundary of mine has been crossed and I try to solve it by being nice, if I am aware, my body tells me there is dissonance. I feel my gut tighten. I bite my bottom lip and hold my breath. When I get alone or my back is turned and no one can see me, I roll my eyes, shake my head in disgust, and make a *tah!* sound through my teeth.

Emotionally: I usually feel resentment and anger. Then a sense of begrudging obligation that I should do it sets in.

Mentally: My first thought when I feel like I'm being manipulated is protest—"Yeah, but" or "What about . . . ?" or "How come . . . ?" or "That's not fair!"—before my desire to avoid conflict kicks in and minimizes the boundary breach with "It's not that big a deal. I'll adjust. What can you expect? People are the worst."

Behavior: I might gossip about the boundary-breacher and make fun of their insane demands behind their back. Because of the built-up resentment, I might get prickly and snippy at someone who has less power than I do (usually my kids, I'm ashamed to say).

Examine

I can't tell you how many times, when I'm working with clients and I ask about what boundaries they can set and hold in order to address a difficult work or personal situation, I receive blank stares and a variation on "I don't know. I've never thought about boundaries before. I've never set boundaries before." Or "I was raised to help people, and I like helping people, so I haven't thought much about boundaries." My guess is that if you were able to finish the quote by Thumper's mother, you were raised, like me, during a time when no one talked about setting boundaries or limits on what worked for you in a relationship and what didn't. You were raised to be . . . nice.

If this is your first time really thinking about boundaries—what they are, how to set them, when to amend them, why you need them (you aren't a bad person for having boundaries)—you are among friends. When I started changing patterns, I realized I had danced with a thousand lies masquerading as truth when it came to establishing and maintaining boundaries. Dance partners like:

- People will think I'm selfish.

- I'm supposed to be nice. Pastors are nice. Women are nice.

- I should like everyone. If I don't, something must be wrong with me.

- If I just turn the other cheek long enough, God will reward me or at least get this figured out.

- If I just turn the other cheek long enough, the

other person will realize their abusive behavior. Guilt will motivate them to change. All will be well.

- People will leave if I set boundaries; they like me because I'm helpful.

- People (especially women) who set boundaries are rigid and hard to be around.

- If I set boundaries, I box myself in.

- If I'm wrong, *such-and-such* horrible thing will happen.

- The other person or people will get really mad, and I'll be worse off than when I started.

- I'll get a reputation for being difficult, a drama queen, or high-maintenance.

I imagine you could add many additional lies to this list. These lies and this cultural pressure are the reason many of us don't have a lot of practice setting boundaries. We've let other people tell us who we should be. Upholding niceness as the standard for good living means we filter everything through the possibility that people might think, "That wasn't a nice thing to do." Or "'Nice' people don't do that." The truth these lies all hide is this: we will like ourselves better when we honor our own boundaries. That isn't to say setting and keeping boundaries is easy at all. But it is life-giving. Once you start living with a healthy sense of yourself and what you find life-giving, respectful, and honoring, you will never want to go back to settling for nice.

Apply the Learning

Thank goodness we know things now from psychological research that our parents and grandparents weren't privy to about raising self-aware children. Learning to set life-giving boundaries starts in childhood. Beyond teaching toddlers to share their toys with others and to keep their hands and legs to themselves, children in many settings are being taught how to advocate for themselves, how to give and receive feedback. We've been working on these skills with our kids, sometimes getting it, sometimes missing the mark and then regrouping. Recently, our son, Jacob, put his boundary-setting into practice.

The backstory: Jacob loves all things with wheels and motors. And when I say "all," I mean *all*. His first word was "go." When he was a toddler, he'd nap with his sweaty little fingers clutching a small model skid steer. When he was a preschooler, I kept a plastic tub in the back of the minivan filled with toy tractors, graders, and cars so we were always ready to create an interstate highway system in any sandlot we came across. He was entranced by train crossings, and riding in Grandpa's combine was the highlight of his preschool days. When I had to get some work done, popping in a *Mighty Machines* video about feller bunchers, sawmills, dump trucks, or balers would always give me a good hour.

Now he loves remote-controlled (RC) cars, airplanes, and boats. I'm fairly certain one day he'll figure out how to turn a cinderblock into a remote-controlled flying fortress for LEGO® people. This love of flying RC planes doesn't produce only elation, however. There are plenty of opportunities for frustration when, for some unknown reason, the planes simply fall out of the sky and crash into unsalvageable parts. Or the plane gets stuck in the neighbor's trees. Or the plane won't take off, and something is wrong with the wires. Fixing, rehabbing, and getting these craft flying again falls to the master builder in our family, my husband, and he can easily spend the bulk of a weekend keeping up with repairs.

One day, Jacob came into the house and told me resolutely he was done flying planes.

"What's going on, honey?"

"Dad got mad when the plane crashed, and Dad said a bad word. I am not going to fly planes with Dad if he gets mad."

And there is the boundary. Fair enough.

I responded, "I wouldn't want to fly planes in that situation either. What would you like to do about it?"

Jacob: "I'm going to tell Dad that the rule is we only have fun while flying planes, and if he gets mad, I'm not flying planes with him."

A good rule for many situations—we only have fun!

We found Tim in the backyard, near the most recent crash site, and as Jacob approached him, Tim took his cue from Jacob's determined stride. He got on a knee to be at eye level with Jacob, who said his piece. Tim put his arm around Jacob and said, "I'm sorry I got angry. I like your rule that flying planes is about having fun." And this is yet another reason I love that man!

Because we've been practicing with our children to state what they need, we were able to stop an incident from becoming a pattern. The beauty of it? Father and son now remind each other, "We don't get mad flying planes. We have fun." There are ample times when the RC Cub crashes into a rock or gets snow stuck in the ailerons, and Jacob is called to live into his own rule.

Our boundaries don't need to be massive, unmovable, or unchangeable. If we think of boundaries this way, then we've created the trinity of death. Then we've caged *ourselves* in. When we change a boundary, we need to be clear in our own head and heart about why we are doing it. Is it coming from a life-giving place that feels like truth? Feels like life? Does the new boundary honor God, others, and ourselves? When we think through our boundaries and find in them a life-giving purpose, bringing accountability to ourselves and others, we are authentically grounded and present in the moment. The more we practice setting and honoring boundaries, the more they become habits, and habits change our lives.

These are some of the life-giving boundaries I now use in my life that a decade ago I would have thought were unrealistic and pie-in-the-sky dreams. Now I won't do life without them:

- If I am not respected in a conversation, I won't continue in it. I will come back to it when it can be respectful.

- I am not going to automatically say yes to volunteering because I think I *should* do the task or because it would look good if I did it. Whatever the job is, if I don't feel called to do it, I will trust that God has gifted and excited someone else to do it. Or maybe it doesn't actually need to be done.

- My passion doesn't have to be your passion. Your passion doesn't have to be mine.

- I turn to curiosity when I've been hurt, instead of psychoanalyzing you.

- I give myself as much love and grace as I give my children. (Be still, shame voices!)

- I won't let the parts of my past that make me cringe define how I show up today or in the future. I will love and learn from those parts.

- When I'm jealous, I will reflect on why. Because I want to do what you are doing? Because I think it would be fun? Because seeing you do it gets me excited, but I've listened too long to the voice that says I shouldn't do that or I don't get to do that? Or am I jealous because I think my life would be better if I had that marble countertop, or I'd be more successful if I had that job? Jealousy can teach us many things, but like garlic, unless it is handled wisely, it will overpower everything else.

- I will not compare my life to the moments shared on someone else's Facebook page. (I cleaned the toilets today. And felt *good*. You sipped wine on the Riviera. You suck. I am now jealous.)

- I will go back to the above boundary on jealousy.

- I will reality-check my expectations of others. This one is huge. I mean, monumental. You live by this boundary and your joy will increase. If I expect you to behave in a way that is life-giving for me, but you have never lived that way in the past, it is unreasonable for me to think you will begin now, unless we have a hard, deep conversation. As wise therapists say, "They have shown you all along who they are. You can believe them."

- I will limit the amount of news I hear and watch. I will be informed but not to the point of being overwhelmed and paralyzed. I don't bring my best to the world when I'm filled with fear that it is going to boil or blow up.

- I will create new traditions with our family.

- We will not spend more than four nights staying in a relative's house. Relatives won't stay more than four nights at our house. You love each other, but five nights is just too long. Love 'em and leave 'em.

- I won't get sucked into my children's emotional states. I don't have to take on their emotional frenzy, and I can be better for them when I am calm, grounded, and have fed my soul.

- I will recognize when I'm numbing myself by doing "good work" (doing the laundry or dishes, cleaning out the basement, writing a grant proposal) instead of doing the priority task.

- I hold my story closely to myself; I don't try to connect by sharing too much too quickly. But when I do share, it will be because I feel a genuine connection with you.

- And it is okay if I feel that genuine connection with fewer people than I would have expected.

You could add many more to this list. I imagine that in another decade, my list will look different, but the point is, boundaries help us know not so much what is coming our way but how we will respond to what is coming. Since I've been living with these boundaries, I have fewer moments when I feel like I just sold myself out. Like I betrayed myself. That I threw myself under the bus. That I broke trust with myself. That I didn't stand up for myself because the "Christian thing" to do would be to patiently wait for someone else to stand up for me. That I should turn the other cheek and accept long-suffering. When I feel like I've sold myself out, I live with greater fear, sadness, and anxiety. But when I rely on my discerned boundaries, I still can get beaten up emotionally and I still can cry a river and slap together adjectives and four-letter words like I'm gunning for the top prize at a creative cussin' contest. (I only swear like this with people I really trust and go to when I'm in shame or pain.) But I hold my head high because I know I'm modeling for my children respect for myself. This modeling is important to me because I want them to respect themselves even when others don't. That's what boundaries are about: Living well. Loving well. Allowing good to be done. Being kind. Bringing our unique best to the world.

Maybe there will be a remake of the *Bambi* movie with a modern twist, and Thumper's mom will still lovingly chide her little bunnies about their manners. But this time instead of saying, "If you can't say anything nice, don't say anything at all," she'll say, "Respect others' boundaries. Know your own. And be kind."

6.

"People Must Like Me"

Integrity

I had always believed that being liked was important. It was a survival strategy in junior high, it made meeting new people easier, it made being a new leader easier, it made life more comfortable . . . or so I thought.

My unexamined thoughts told me that if I (1) agreed with other people, (2) allowed myself to be molded into whoever I thought they'd prefer I be, (3) kept quiet, (4) turned the other cheek, and (5), with the smoothness of a 1950s beauty queen, diverted conflictual topics with a somewhat flirty "You have nothing to fear here" response, I would get people to like me.

I wasn't intentionally being deceptive; I just wanted to be liked and to avoid judgment. My experiences growing up had taught me that conflict didn't usually end well, and the model I learned for managing conflict wasn't healthy. You tried hard to avoid conflict, and if you did find yourself in it, you worked your way through it by taking more responsibility than was yours to take. Hiding from taking responsibility was an option too. If people liked me, I thought the fact that I dealt with conflict this way was part of *why* they liked me. Being likable was synonymous with being agreeable. It didn't occur to me that people might *still* like me even if I disagreed with them, even if I shared my opinion about conflictual topics. I thought I had cracked the "stay safe" code—even though it required selling myself out. Could I have stayed safe *and* stayed true to myself?

That never occurred to me. Not even once.

The lie that people must like me was a really hard one for me to recognize. Cognitively, I knew the notion that "if you make people like you, things will turn out" isn't always true, but the lie lived in my bones. It is a lie I still have to debunk. Every. Day.

So, to bring you up to speed: for many reasons, in the first congregation I served the conditions were right for an explosive conflict that pushed the limits of this lie. First of all, our denomination, the Evangelical Lutheran Church in America (ELCA), was actively discerning through study, prayer, and discussions within congregations, synods, and the national church whether the ELCA would ordain people in the LGBTQIA+ community. This question quickly raised crucial questions about biblical authority: *How* does one read the Bible, and what does it *mean* for us? These conversations needed to happen, but by participating in them, some churches experienced conflict among pastoral teams, among members, between clergy and members, and between the congregation and the larger church. These were difficult, raw, painful times. At synod assemblies for almost the first decade after I was ordained, this topic was hotly debated. I look back now and think how courageous and loving people in the LGBTQIA+ community were to show up again and again at these synod assemblies and have their personhood debated.

As if this issue were not enough, local circumstances compounded the tensions. The congregation I was serving was nearing the fiftieth anniversary of its founding, a time of identity crisis and transition for many churches. Membership was declining, and while the congregation was still large, a sense of anxiety about the future had set in. Additionally, three new pastors began serving the congregation within eighteen months after it had been served for nearly fifty years by only two senior pastors. And maybe all along there had been a mismatch between some members (the old guard) and the new pastoral leadership. Maybe it was just a matter of time until tension, distrust, gossip, and anxiety filled pews and hearts.

Anxiety, back-channeling (the meeting after the meeting), and gossip became codified when a group of about fifteen couples, many of whom had been friends for decades, got together and compiled a document listing everything they'd like to see changed. The document covered theology (more preaching about hell, for example), worship planning, financial management, and personnel issues. The church executive team brought in a consultant to help us effectively manage and respond to these concerns. We had special congregational meetings and "cottage meetings" (smaller meetings in people's homes). Council members resigned because of the stress. Some congregational members quietly found new churches, while others rallied to show support for the current leadership. So many people were negatively affected. Personally, I felt anxious every time I pulled into the church parking lot. I was newly pregnant at the height of the conflict, and as a congregational annual meeting attended by hundreds of people carried on for five hours, I wondered how all the tension would affect our baby. As midnight approached, I felt absolutely despondent and started wondering if I could patch together an income teaching piano lessons and cleaning houses.

It was a long, stressful fifteen months. Still, other than the man who told my husband (without knowing it was my husband he was talking to—*Oops! Awk-ward!*) that I should go back to North Dakota because I didn't belong at this church as a pastor, until this conflict really heated up, I felt like I'd had fairly good relationships with the members at the lead of the issue. The concerned members and I weren't buddies, like being in a card club together or exchanging muffin recipes, but I would have said that we had positive relationships. I would even have said they found me likable.

I had been intentional about not sharing too much of my personality (my goofy, edgier side—I was going for more of a Kate Middleton classy calm) or my personal life with members of the congregation. This kept me in control of my public image and felt safer to me. I had tried consciously to cultivate relationships and activities outside of the church because, as many pastors will tell you, being friends with your parishioners is tricky at best and often problematic. To navigate friendships with members successfully, you have to be very good at maintaining boundaries. I simply chose to navigate this by mostly keeping my church relationships and my friend relationships separate. I was friendly, kind to people, but on Friday night, if Tim and I were going to throw a party, we'd be inviting friends we'd had for years, people from outside the church.

It was at the wedding of one of those friends I'd had for years that my worlds collided, and my neat, simplistic understanding of the grumpers as mean-spirited and manipulative was challenged. I did not like it. I did not like my personal world serving as a real-life example of "two degrees of separation." The reception seating was open, and we arrived later than most of our friends. As a result, we had to sit at a table with friends of friends of friends, all around our age. Given the emotional state I was already in, meeting new people and explaining what I did professionally was an unwelcome chore, but at least this would be a respite from the tension that currently marked large-group gatherings for me.

Or so I thought. Who did I end up sitting next to? Out of all the 3.3 million people in the Twin Cities? Out of all the 150 people at the reception? Out of the ten people around our table? Who?

Whoooo?

The *next-door neighbor* of one of the chief grumpers.

What is the freakin' probability of *that*?

Sweet mother of pearl. Why don't ya just poke me in the eye with a stick?

This whole love-fest kicked off when he introduced himself and asked what I did.

"I'm a pastor."

Not hard to imagine what the next reasonable question would be—"Where?"—which he asked and I answered. And that quickly led him to remember that the elderly man who loaned him rakes and shovels while pleasantly chatting over the fence went to this church, and by chance, did I know him? Strike up "It's a small world after all. . . . It's a word of laughter, a world of tears." Well, isn't that sardonically true?

When we made this connection, unchurchy, uncharitable thoughts filled my head, which started to pound. My back stiffened, my gut tightened, my cheeks flushed, and I dug my nails into my palms and . . . smiled at this chirpy next-door neighbor, who was enjoying his garden salad. It was all I had in me to stay in that chair for the rest of the reception. I didn't feel safe, and I was filled with anger. The devil must be tormenting me. The devil or God. Sometimes it is hard to tell. (The six-syllable phrase for this theological mystery is *Deus absconditus*—"hidden God").

I knew our mutual connection as a person who was

judgmental, who complained, and who had masterminded an entire alternative slate to the nominated church council candidates. I knew him as a bully who blustered and gave ominous warnings in a grave voice: "There is no room in the church for gay pastors." Before the conflict began, he scared me, and I much preferred interacting with his wife—the kind who smiled and patted your arm. He was the kind who shook my hand too aggressively and was terse. During the conflict, he—along with other grumps—haunted my dreams.

And now, apparently, he got to haunt my date nights too. But it gets better. We're not done yet. The pinnacle of this supper was when the next-door neighbor paused and, with all sincerity, said, "Isn't he just the nicest guy?"

No, no. Actually, just, no. My experience is different from yours. I've experienced him to be an arrogant bully.

There was so much I wanted to say. But I'm a pastor. A pastor in every situation. A pastor who must master how to avoid a disaster. No room for honesty or a differing opinion, and don't I need to uphold the eighth commandment?

"Isn't he just the nicest guy?"

. . . *how to avoid a disaster.*

Plastering on a smile, I nodded and said, "That is great to hear! Isn't it great to have great neighbors?" He gave me a quizzical look that said, "I really don't get what you just said because that isn't a normal response, but maybe you're not as normal as I thought you were."

And then I focused on cleaning up my plate of asparagus-stuffed chicken so I wouldn't have to talk. The problem was that I was so deeply hurt and so pissed off. I've since learned that anger is usually a secondary emotion. What comes first is grief or fear, and I was doggy-paddling through fear and anxiety every single day.

Whatever I was being asked to do or learn that night was simply too big of an ask. I wasn't ready to give up my version of the grumpers, because to do so—to allow additional, differing information into my assessment of them—would have left me adrift with little way to understand what was happening at church. I probably would have become even moodier, wondering, *If these people are so great, what about this situation at our church is so off? What about us as pastors is so off?* I was trapped in my understanding of who these people were, and it wasn't until many years later, when I was emotionally calm enough to honestly see their capacity for both kindness and chaos, that I was able to hold on to both "Yes, he could be a great neighbor" and "Yes, in my opinion, his behavior in our faith community was destructive." Both things could be true.

This wedding wasn't the only time my professional and personal worlds collided. I had been taking voice lessons for a few years by the time the conflict started. I liked the technical challenge of performing at a high level, and I loved learning new music. This fed my soul. I took voice lessons at a large conservatory serving the entire Minneapolis/St. Paul area. This was the place to go if you wanted your preschooler to learn drumming or your kindergartner to get started on Suzuki violin, or if you were an aspiring performer brushing up on your skills in opera or musical theater. Two hundred-forty faculty members teaching in thirty-five concentrations provided literally thousands of lessons in this seven-story brownstone each week. Of course, hundreds of lessons each week meant hundreds of students coming and going at their assigned lesson times.

So who was the shy tween whose lesson followed mine? *Whoooo? Whooo-oooo?* The granddaughter of the chiefest grumper of them all. Yet again, I was forced to play "two degrees of separation" when the only game I wanted to play was darts, which gave me something to do with my anger. I figured out this connection when the tween's mom was waiting during the tween's lesson, and I was bundling up in my coat, boots, and mittens for the Minnesota cold. Because the roster of students and lesson times was posted on the instructor's door and because my name was right above her daughter's, the mom figured out that I was the pastor at her mother- and father-in-law's church.

"Are you the pastor at their church? Isn't my mother-in-law so sweet?"

Oh, farts in a truck. You have *got* to be *freakin'* kidding me.

I was sick of playing nice, and the song "Not Ready to Make Nice" by the Dixie Chicks had become my go-to song. The Dixie Chicks were battling out how real and authentic they could be with their political views in the country music world, and at the time this song came out, based on the number of radio stations that had pulled their music, the country music world appeared to be winning. I stood with my Dixie Chicks. I was not ready to make nice either. I wasn't going to say she was so sweet. Nope. Not today. But I couldn't be a jerk, so I did what I've done masterfully a hundred times before. The divert-and-redirect. "Oh my gosh! Isn't that funny! What a small world! Funny! Now, how old is your daughter? How does she like lessons? Oh, I know the teacher is great. Just great."

And then I hustled to the elevator.

Even that wasn't the end of it. On a pleasant spring evening, the studio recital was held in a beautiful park pavilion by one of Minnesota's 10,000 lakes. As is the tradition with recitals, the younger, less experienced performers go first, and the more experienced performers sing at the end. This put me at the end of the program. It put the granddaughter close to the beginning. Before the recital started, the grandma walked in. Of course she would be there, but my body told me to flee and avoid her. She smiled and tried to talk to me, but at that point I knew only a one-note song, "Panic," on a high B. I excused myself, saying something like that I needed to check in with the accompanist or go warm up or go to the bathroom (I was five months pregnant, after all).

Is it totally wrong of me to admit that I took a bit of pleasure in hearing the granddaughter sing? In hearing warbling notes, flat pitches, and missed entrances? In comparing how I remembered I sang at age eleven with her ability? Is it totally wrong that I approached that recital as a showdown, pulling out my arpeggios, open vowels, and sustained high As when my competition—unknowingly standing in for her grumpy grandfather in my mind—was still learning the state capitals? And is it totally wrong that after I performed, I smugly—yet humbly, always look humble—sat down and congratulated myself that I had kicked some ass? I couldn't kick it in church. I couldn't kick it on social media (that didn't exist, and I wouldn't have done that if it had). I couldn't kick it in words. But, damn, I could crush it on the stage with a voice that was far more powerful than my size and demeanor would suggest.

Vocal smackdown, thank you very much.

And is it totally wrong that when the granddaughter came up to tell me she liked my song, I lied and told her she did a good job and I really liked her song too?

That was the only part I got right. Yes, I know these weren't kind thoughts. I knew it at the time. But when you feel like you are voiceless and you feel so strongly that what you need more than anything else is to have a voice that can make your life better—or at least free from conflict and emotional abuse—you express that need through any means you can.

Which is a truth with which the grumpers would probably concur. They would probably have said they felt the same way. The church they helped found was slowly losing members. And a view some of them held as truth—"Homosexuality is a sin"—was being challenged. And a new theological understanding was emerging about human sexuality. And with that new understanding, new practices of ordination were being put forth. And their adult children were very lax about getting their grandchildren baptized and didn't bring the little ones to Sunday school. And all this created anxiety for them, and they, too, were looking for a way to give voice to all that anxiety. They, too, might have said something like "Is it totally wrong if some gossip and insinuation gets the job done? Is it totally wrong that we lose our tempers if we save our church? Is it totally wrong if we appear intimidating but keep the church following the inerrant Word of God?"

During the conflict, there were many times when one of them would pull me aside and say, "You know, we aren't talking about *you*," as criticism was hurled at the other pastors. Tim and I called this "the pink bubble." I could go into the pink bubble of protection, keep smiling, not having opinions of my own—or having only the opinions that were already sanctioned. Buying into the lie that people must like me. Yet, that didn't feel authentic because I loved the pastoral colleagues I worked with, and I had heard stories of how pastoral teams could easily turn on each other. We weren't going to be another chapter in that story. So I chose to stand outside of the bubble.

The evening when twenty-five people came to observe

the council meeting, I probably made this clear. As we moved through the agenda, some of the observers moved from observing into commenting. As I recall, one of my pastoral colleagues commented on the comment, and an exchange started. It seemed to me that the observer was being disrespectful by omitting the earned title "Pastor" with my female colleague. We hadn't been adamant, correcting people to use "Pastor," but we did model it for the congregation, referring to each other as Pastor Karl, Pastor Stella, and Pastor Sarah. The observer repeatedly called her by only her first name. Out of a depth unknown to me, without thinking about the impact, simply responding in anger and indignation when he addressed her again with just her first name, I interrupted him and said, "*Pastor* Stella." To which he shot back, "Well, if she's *Pastor*, then I'm *Mr.* Thompson." My anger had spurred on his anger. That didn't calm things down, but it did shock the room into silence until the council president suggested we take a break. During which I quickly went and apologized to Mr. Thompson. The pink bubble was calling to me; I still needed Mr. Thompson to like me.

Finding My Way to Truth: Integrity

Being likable only takes you so far. When relationships break down and the lie we have believed is that people must like us, an emotional quandary sets in. We can know it is an *emotional* quandary when we feel taken advantage of or resentful, thinking, *I was nice—what more do they want?* It is time to pop our bubbles.

Pay Attention

While it is hard to do, we must develop awareness about what we are thinking, what we are feeling, and how we are behaving if we want to move forward as a whole, integrated person regardless of whether the relationship itself is healed. When we pay attention, we start to see patterns in ourselves that are second nature and may need to change. We begin to change them by *seeing* them.

When I started working through the emotional impact of this painful church conflict, I saw how the lie that I needed people to like me had limited me. I had embraced this lie as a subconscious leadership strategy, and while it worked for a while, when things became difficult, it didn't work. It didn't prevent me from feeling pain and anger. In fact, I carried pain for years after I left this congregation. I remember walking into a chain restaurant located several suburbs over from the church a few months after I'd left. I saw two of my former church adversaries thanking the host, putting their coats on to leave, and I'm sure what I experienced was a panic attack. At the time I didn't have those words to describe what was happening (nor would I have admitted it), but I felt physically unsafe, my heart raced, and my only thought was "I need to leave. I need to get out of here right now." Other times, I couldn't say three sentences about the fifteen-month conflict without feeling physical fury. And the more I talked about it, the angrier I became. Not until I started paying attention did I realize that I had never thought trying to be likable could make me so angry.

Examine

It finally took getting into therapy years later for me to be able not just to *feel* my feelings but to reflect on them. Simply feeling them again hadn't moved me forward; it had kept me stuck. I was in bondage to that lie that I could somehow control people if they liked me. When I examined these strong emotions, I started to truly heal.

To really unpack my emotions, I first needed to increase my ability to be calm through centering prayer, deep breathing, and self-compassion practices. Once I had these tools and a good therapist, I saw things I hadn't recognized before. For example, believing the lie that people must like me prevented me from seeing that the grumpers could be likable people in other contexts. In my anger and hurt, I developed tunnel vision, and all I could see was how terrible they were. I couldn't see that they, too, had complicated personalities. I couldn't see that perhaps in another context, I could be just as destructive as I thought they were. I didn't recognize that my snippiness with the phone company's customer service rep was the same type of life-sucking behavior I had seen in the grumpers at church. If you had said to me during that time that maybe we were *all* wounded and hurting people and that none of us consistently brought integrity and our best selves to situations, I would have wished a thousand slow, painful deaths on you. *I* could be kind to my friends, young children, elders, and strangers *and* be mean-spirited in my thoughts about the concerned church members. Therefore, when I made mean, vast generalizations about the grumpers to my father-in-law, I felt justified in my judgments. After all, *I* was the victim.

Apply the Learning

Many good books have been written on dealing with church conflict. What I am offering here is a look at one's own emotional process and reactivity. When we can see how our own processing of an event limits us or keeps us stuck, we gain emotional freedom to forgive ourselves and others. I now have grace and emotional calm to look back over almost fifteen years and say, "Those were painful times, but lots of good people tried for good outcomes. I am grateful for those people. We all struggled, and it was hard for everyone involved. And those who were the chief adversaries were doing the best they could at the time." As a sensitive, heart-centered person, this is a monumental thing for me to say authentically. I *do* have goodwill for them. Looking back, I see that we were more alike than I cared to admit at the time. We *all* have the capacity for both kindness and destruction.

I now have greater perspective into how I got tripped up by believing that people liking me was an indicator of my success. I see the "People must like you" lie faster now, and it carries less importance than it did, but I can get sucked back into it before I know it has happened. What helps immensely is working on self-compassion and healthy boundaries; both strengthen my integrity. This means treating people with kindness and respect, but remembering that it is okay for not everyone to like me, even if I do treat them well. I don't like everyone either!

What is my motivation for treating people with kindness and respect? My internal sense of integrity. Do you see how the motive shifts? No longer am I driven to get a desired outcome from *you*; rather, my actions are grounded in what is real and authentic for *me*. In day-to-day living, the actions would be the same either way. *But* when conflict comes or a hard decision needs to be made, that internal shift will guide me to live and lead authentically, and I believe that produces better outcomes.

Conflict is part of leading, but how we engage in conflict is a choice.

This conflict happened fourteen years ago, and there are things I'd do differently if I knew then what I know now. I've wondered how my ministry there equipped people in their faith. Did it matter that I was there? Recently I ran into a member of this congregation who, unprompted, said, "Your ministry touched a lot of people." I had wondered what my time meant in that place, and I also wondered in that moment if the individual was just being nice, but she went on to say something very specific: "You were with us. You didn't stand away from us. You showed us your vulnerabilities."

For years I had tried to get people to like me by avoiding being real—by quickly adapting to what I thought others expected, by highlighting or minimizing parts of myself, by not letting them see too much or know me too fully—in an effort to control their perception of me. Yet, here was this woman of the same generation as the concerned members saying that what she remembered was that I showed my imperfections and struggles, my humanness. She believed my time there touched a lot of people, because I was vulnerable. Maybe she was thinking of the time I dropped the mic—literally, and on a tile floor—while presiding at Holy Communion. Or the time I started to do a baptism before realizing there was no water in the font. Or the times I cried while preaching because God's goodness and love had swept me up. All times when I couldn't present a best version of myself.

Maybe, just maybe, this kind woman shared these words with me not because I'd gotten her to like me all those years ago but simply because, from her perspective and at that time, they were true.

7.

"I'm Responsible for It All"

Hope

I can already hear the pushback about this lie: "But I *am* responsible for it all. I *am* the leader. The buck *does* stop with me. It is *my* license on the line." I get it. Leadership does require us to be responsible, it does require us to problem-solve, to be solution focused, to empower others, to strive for positive outcomes. But are you exhausted some of the time? Stressed almost all of the time? Do intrusive thoughts about what didn't get done at work pop into your head when you are supposed to be relaxing or having fun with friends? Are you terse with your family? Resentful that you are working harder than everyone else? If you answered yes to more than one or two of these questions, know there are a million of us experiencing the very same thing right now. Hang in there with me. It can get better. I promise.

Let's start with a story. Becoming parents kicked our butts. True, my medical chart did include the words "geriatric pregnancy" and "advanced maternal age," so that must indicate we would have had more energy for the sleepless nights if we had been a decade younger. And true, we did live far from family who could pop over to watch the baby for the evening. But Tim, Chiara, and I struggled together and against each other those first four months of her life. When we would finally get her to sleep, Tim and I would *stay up* to argue about who was getting more sleep. I called him a few times at work to say, "Whatever you are doing is easier than what I'm doing." Then I'd let Chiara wail for a few seconds and hang up. One might say I was harassing him, but I liked to think of it as reminding him of who had it better. And then there was the time he was in the checkout lane at the grocery store, starting to bag the items he'd gathered, when I called and implored him to get home *right now*. "Just leave the food! I need you home!" It was the hardest time in our marriage.

To get Chiara to stop crying, we ran the vacuum, bounced for hours on the exercise ball, shushed like "the angriest librarian you've ever heard"—that phrase from a baby book is seared into my memory, probably because every time I did that, I became light-headed and almost passed out. We learned seven variations of swaddling and called her our baby burrito. We mastered the technique of vigorously—yet not *too* vigorously—rocking her on our laps between our knees. We let her sleep in our arms. We pinned one of my stinky T-shirts to her mattress so she felt comforted when we laid her down. We walked her in the baby carrier. And when there was no relief, I'd cry right along with her. Part of why we didn't have children earlier was because I was pretty certain I wouldn't make a good mom, and those first few months seemed to me to confirm that. On the fourth day home from the hospital, I told my mom, who had driven twelve hours to help us, that I was sure Chiara didn't like me. My mom took her from my arms and said, "I think you need to get some sleep." Interestingly, it seemed clear that Chiara liked me when I woke up more three hours later.

But when Chiara cried, she didn't *just* cry; she wailed at the top of her lungs. It seemed like she felt responsible for everything that was wrong, like she had been born to bear the weight of the world on her little shoulders, that somehow the job of carrying the pain of all that was so, so unjust and destructive was hers to do. She howled like her charge in life was to give voice to all those whose voices had been silenced by abuse, war, and terror.

Of course, that was my theological, emotional perspective on what was happening—like she was the baby version of the wailing prophet Jeremiah. All the baby books pointed to colic (which I had had as a child) or a less severe form of distress called "extreme fussiness," which she would eventually grow out of. But that was of little comfort when she wailed through her whole baptism and we missed most of the service because I was in the narthex with her, swaddling and rocking and shushing.

Like an angry librarian.

As a leader, do you relate to Chiara's agony at least a little bit? Maybe all the crying is because you are a small-business owner and for the past six months, you have been taking out loans to make payroll—"What's another hundred thou'?" Or maybe you've shut your door and cried because you just had to lay off a really good employee. Or the bond agency lowered the city's Triple A rating, the first time in twenty-three years, and it was on your watch. Or even with all the training and retraining, a student with known physical aggression still beat up a teacher who is now hospitalized. Or the health inspectors just arrived, and you have no emotional reserve for that today. There are a hundred reasons for us to cry behind closed doors or on the drive to work or on the light rail at the end of the day—because for many of us in leadership, there are literally a hundred things that, if they go wrong today will go *really* wrong—and it will be on our watch. It will be our responsibility. This sense of potential catastrophe is captured in the adage "Being the administrator of a nursing home [*or insert another leadership role here*] is like driving a ship filled with gunpowder through a shower of sparks."

Maybe you don't relate to the tears so much, but you do have the sense that you truly *are* responsible for it all: having all the answers, fixing and righting inherited systems that haven't worked well for the past thirty years, making something really great come together, pulling off the family reunion without drama as the main thing people take away from the weekend.

I assume we all want to do a good job, at least most of the time. What is yours to be responsible for? And what is not?

One pastor recently told me what several more echoed: "As a pastor, I feel like I have to have all the answers." From how to pronounce that seven-syllable name of some unknown son in the tribe of Naphtali, to how to get the young people to come back to church, to what the warranty on the boiler is, to who still needs to turn in their permission slips for summer camp, to how to put broken families back together again at the deathbed of the family matriarch.

What is yours to be responsible for? And what is not? The lie that we are responsible for it all—having all the answers, solving the problems (global and local), and moving mission forward—is alive and well because being responsible seems like a good thing, right? And who wants to follow a leader who isn't sure where they are going?

I was working with a leadership team for a company that had grown from six to more than eighty employees in three years. People who had technical expertise had been promoted to director positions and were now in charge of leading teams. They talked about the pressure to have all the answers and the guilt and worry they felt if they couldn't troubleshoot the legalities of some obscure situation, or if they couldn't remember all the steps of a specific protocol, or if they couldn't articulate the organization's vision for changes that were being implemented. They all agreed that when they didn't know the answers, or when their subordinates or colleagues seemed annoyed that they couldn't quickly resolve a situation, or when they had to redirect or reprimand or correct an employee—they wondered if maybe they weren't the right person for the job, maybe they couldn't do the role they had been promoted to. This worry chipped away at their self-confidence, creating a self-fulfilling cycle. If that cycle of a troublesome issue, worry, and reduced self-confidence goes round and round, the decrease in our self-confidence negatively impacts our ability to see options. It diminishes our ability to find creative solutions, thus reinforcing the lie that we can't lead well because we have to be responsible for finding the answer and we're not succeeding in that. This cycle can throw us off our game quickly, and even though we may still be showing up physically, we aren't bringing our best.

None of the new directors wanted their department to be viewed as the weak link. These newly promoted supervisors all agreed with the one who said, "I feel like when one of my employees messes up or doesn't do a good job, that it reflects negatively on me." How did that affect them? The weight of the whole world—or at least their organization—seemed to be balanced on their shoulders. It increased their sense of responsibility. How many times had they quickly scanned the employee files stored in their brains when a mistake happened to make sure they had provided the proper training? To make sure they had covered this? And then the new directors and I talked about what to do with things you understand to be common sense—like locking up the building at night, or locking up the wine in the church, or double-checking that information was sent to parents and guardians—but when other people who report to you don't treat these matters as common sense.

It seems to me we can clear up some of the emotional debris if we get clear on answers to a few key questions: What really is my responsibility? How do I empower others to take responsibility? How emotionally wrapped up am I in the perceptions of my subordinates or team? What is actually being asked of me in this situation? Who can help me, mentor me? Clarity about these issues takes down the lie that I should be able to do it all on my own—that I should already have figured this out or should hide what I don't know. Clarity reveals that when we hide our lack of knowledge, that is when things can go really wrong really quickly.

When we are unclear in our responses to these questions, we often make rash decisions out of a desire to alleviate uncomfortable emotions. Think of a baby who is crying inconsolably. I know that when I'm around an infant who is wailing, three minutes can feel like thirty and it is excruciating. I just want the baby to stop crying, and I feel helpless when it won't. I would do just about anything to stop the crying and, thus, alleviate my stress response. Leadership can feel the same way: we just want to stop the emotional uncertainty, so we'll do nearly anything to get beyond it. We might make decisions without thinking them through or praying about them. We might zigzag—deciding, reversing decisions, ignoring the problem, reactively deciding again—instead of moving steadily toward our goal. Having an answer, doing something—anything—can make us feel better in the moment simply because it reduces the intense feeling of being stuck or powerless. But what feels better in the moment might not be ideal in the long run.

On the flip side, sometimes we function out of emotional avoidance when we are unclear about our responsibility. Think again of listening to a crying baby. It is stressful! Some of us will just leave the room—and even the house—and let another person calm the child. It is like we forget any experience or knowledge we might have about baby care. When we lead by avoidance, it's often because we feel *responsible* but we don't feel *empowered* to actually dig in. I know this is alive and well in my brain when I'm thinking before a big meeting, *I'll figure this out when I get there. I can wing it. I'll just see how the meeting goes. I'll see what other people want to talk about. So-and-so will probably hijack the meeting, and that's okay because then we won't actually have to make a decision.* I can let this sort of thinking wander all over the place in the guise of brainstorming, discussion, and getting everyone's input. But actually, I'm practicing avoidance because I haven't learned how to say, "What you're saying is important, and we will get to it, but today we need to focus on X, Y, and Z." I haven't gotten clear on what is my responsibility and what isn't. For instance, when I'm clear that I'm the convener and about what that means, I recognize that I am responsible for the structure of the meeting, for providing a clear agenda, for keeping the conversation on task, and for clarifying who is going to do what once the meeting is over. If these are my tasks, I'd better do them because they are my responsibility.

When we get clear on our responsibilities and what is ours to own, we can better support our colleagues. I remember quite well the first Sunday in Advent 2004. The reason I remember this particular Sunday is that I overslept. When you are a preacher, oversleeping on a

Sunday morning is the stuff nightmares are made of. As soon as I opened my eyes, I knew I was in trouble, because it was light out. It shouldn't be light out in freakin' *Minnesota* at the end of November . . . unless you are waking up at 8:36. The worship service had started at 8:30 and, to up the stakes, I was the preacher. I jumped out of bed, saying some of my most unchurchy words in an operatic voice (I squawk in a high-pitched frenzy when I'm on anxiety overload). The landline was ringing, and it was the co-senior pastors—my bosses—calling to see what was happening. Tim was saying I'd be right there. Apparently, as they were calling me, they were also rummaging through their files of old sermons looking for an "Advent 1, year A" sermon they could preach.

I flew out the door. The custodian met me at the church entrance, my alb, cincture, and stole in hand. I got my liturgical wear on while dashing through the basement activity room. I heard special music being piped through the sound system. That was a good sign—I still had time. I ran through the sacristy, slid into the preacher's pew, and listened to sixteen seconds more of music. I still remember who sang the solo that day. I got up, read the Gospel, and preached. After the service, as I was greeting people at the door as they left, several worshippers made remarks like "You sure look different today." Ya think? I didn't have my contacts in, no makeup, I'd finger-brushed my hair in the car. Oh, and I didn't have any tights or nylons on. Sporting very pale legs is something you do in April or May in the Upper Midwest, but the end of November? In Minnesota? That definitely advertised that something had gone awry.

Public failures are things I really try to avoid. I'd much prefer to hide my foibles or control the presentation of them. So my self-talk while dashing and zipping around that morning was filled with shame and self-blame: "You are an impostor pastor. They all hate you. You are a f***-show with a side of s**t salad." While preaching I had to force myself to look at people, because my mind was so busy making up stories about their faces. "They hate me. See, just look at that. They know I overslept. I disgust them." My theater background is what got me through; you can sing and dance your way through pretty much anything. The show (or in this case, the sermon) must go on.

I was in a shame storm, feeling so awful about myself, and the faces of everyone who had ever been mean to me filled my head to affirm my self-assessment. The hot guy from summer camp who told me I wasn't good-looking, mean girls from high school—you get the idea. During the offertory, one of the senior pastors walked through the sacristy, slid into the preacher pew beside me, and with all earnestness and grace said, "Thanks for being here, and thanks for your words."

Oh, thank God I get to work with you.

After worship I apologized a zillion times, and by the time we got in our cars after the second service, all was well. This is a story I will treasure for as long as I have cognitive ability to recall it, because his few words taught me so much about grace, kindness, and responsibility. He knew what was his and what wasn't. He was grounded enough in himself to not tie his ego up in having people believe he "ran a tight ship." Furthermore, he could look at the evidence: oversleeping was a one-off. I hadn't done it before, and I've never overslept when preaching or leading worship since. He knew I was responsible, because my actions generally demonstrated that.

Here's the thing about empathy and grace: if he hadn't given me kindness in that moment, I don't know if I'd be telling this story—at least not with as much transparency as

I am—because shame would own that story. Shame would have owned me in that moment with never a thought that there might be different ways of understanding what had happened. But he gave me kindness that sent the message "Hey, I know you got this. On we go." The beauty is that on Tuesday at the staff meeting, no one poked at my vulnerability. No one joked, "Hey! I almost called you this morning." Or "Awesome! You are right on time!" I wasn't called into his office to work through a correction plan. That wasn't needed.

I did make a mistake. I messed up. This is the pastor version of missing a big client pitch, or missing a medication pass, or getting three weeks into the quarter before realizing a student's Individualized Education Plan had not been followed. In the church world, my oversleeping on a Sunday morning was a big deal. I imagine several other senior pastors would have responded differently. And truly, if I were leading a congregation, I would probably want to pummel the one who caused the stress I'd experienced while rummaging for an old sermon as the prelude was playing. I can't honestly say I would respond as kindly as my co-senior pastor did. I'd like to live into his example, but I don't know that I'm there yet.

When I've shared this story with others who have served as associate pastors, they remind me how fortunate I was that Pastor Karl responded this way. But most of us, even in the church, just might want our "pound of flesh" because we believe we need to solve every situation, or at least place some blame. He didn't want or need a pound of flesh because he had a clear understanding of who he was and how he was fulfilling the call of senior pastor. Upholding people's integrity and humanity was core to how he led. And you know what? His kindness to me and his sense of clear boundaries around what and wasn't his made me the most loyal of subordinates. I would have followed him into a burning building . . . or at least into a massive church conflict.

Finding My Way to Truth: Hope

The biggest consequence of believing the lie "I am responsible for it all" is that we flicker out, burn out, or work out our s**t on other people. We snap at people. But my co-senior pastor didn't do any of those things. Instead, he modeled hope that this would work out too—that my mistake wasn't the end of the world, like my shame was telling me it was—and that on we would go.

Pay Attention

When I overslept that Sunday morning, I felt fear, shame, and guilt. As I zipped around grabbing my clothes, I was swearing and angry. I blamed myself for being in a profession where my failures would be so public. After the service, I felt sheepish and wanted to avoid people. For the next few days, I anticipated that my oversleeping would blow up into something bigger than it was.

Examine

As leaders, we simplify our inner life immensely when we get clear about what we are and are not responsible for. We can be responsible for a lot, but as soon as we get sucked into believing the lie that we are responsible for it *all*, we start micromanaging, we over-function, we take ownership for things that aren't ours—and we don't pause to reflect on and integrate experiences we've had that prove we are not and cannot be responsible for it all. We make reactive, rash decisions, maybe overpromising or saying yes too quickly. Then we have to figure out how to deliver on that promise, which inevitably feels too similar to parallel-parking an F-150 pickup. Downtown. During rush hour. It takes a whole lot of maneuvering and squeezing, only to return from a nice dinner to find that a Volkswagen Beetle has blocked you in and you are stuck going nowhere.

Some problems we simply cannot fix on our own, and we deceive ourselves when we function like we can. Like we can be the savior (and we'll get lots of kudos if we can be the savior), or at least die trying (but that's a pretty big expense). I'm not talking about regulatory compliance or following the established protocols. I'm talking about the more nuanced, complicated, entrenched problems, the dandelions of the leadership garden. If it feels like no matter how hard you dig around the root or how much you spray that problem dandelion, it just pops back up, call trusted colleagues into that garden to help you. You don't have to do this alone. It is absolutely okay to ask for help. Really.

Sometimes the best thing we can do as leaders is simply name that a problem exists—to recognize that the problem is there, and to attend to it by listening with empathy, being curious to see what path forward will emerge, and doing what we can—not more, not less. Church closings come to mind. Sometimes simply prayerfully attending and naming what we see as leaders is the most honest—though often the hardest—thing we can do.

Apply the Learning

Years ago, when our baby wasn't able to stop crying, Tim was a grounded and calm dad because he seemed to have figured out what he could and couldn't do to solve the problem. As Chiara wailed, he would hold her up to eye level and look at her scrunched-up, red, distressed face, smile at her, and say, "Do you know what we do with little babies who cry? Do you know? We kiss 'em."

And then he'd cover her little face with loud smooches and kiss those tears and hug her tight.

It was so tender, so present . . . so hopeful. Her tears still came, as if she were solely responsible for all that was wrong in the world. Tim's words didn't fix the sense that she was called to bear the burdens of the whole world through her tears. But a transformation happened—in Tim. And in me. Tim could be with her in the pain. He'd take it away if he could in a heartbeat, but when he couldn't, he would cover that pain with love. No amount of anxiety and turmoil was going to push him away. Through his actions he would embody hope that tomorrow or the tomorrow after that would be better. That we'd get this figured out. That we would be in the struggle together—not against each other but *with* each other. That these were moments—as hard as they were. They were *moments*, and moments pass.

"What do we do with little babies who cry? . . . We kiss 'em."

In those dark days of sleep deprivation, this small action on Tim's part helped us live into our infant's name, Chiara Hope. In Italian, *Chiara* means "bright or shining." Bright Hope. Shining Hope. We knew life would bring struggle, so we always wanted hope to be not only the center of her name but the grounding of her life. Little did we know before she was born that hope was also what we, her parents, would need in those first months.

Maybe after reading this chapter you feel disheartened because you realize, again, that your job responsibilities truly are too much for one person. Many of us are in positions like that. When this happens, we need to have a different conversation, one about exploring how to right-size your responsibilities, about who can help, about whether this over-work is temporary, about what else you might like to do with your skills. Or maybe after reading this chapter you are stymied: patterns of taking responsibility for everything are so entrenched in your thinking and working that you wonder how gaining clarity about what is and isn't yours can bring life-giving and hopeful change. No doubt, changing patterns is hard work, and reinforcement is needed. I've felt defeated or slipped back into old habits many times. But hope reminds us that even a small shift in direction dramatically changes where a ship ends up. Hope says we get to captain our ship. Hope says we can learn from today's mistakes, and can be better and do better tomorrow. Hope is active, not passive. Hope is what we have when we believe we can change our lives and then get specific about how to do that. Hope is one of the most powerful things a leader can provide for their team.

Hope will bring us home emotionally. Hope will get us through. Hope reminds us that we aren't responsible for everything. We are responsible for our part—our "bit," as they say in England. Hope reminds us that even when all evidence seems to the contrary, God is working for life and for good.

8.

"I Need to Be the Right Type of Christian"

Authenticity

I've often been told either clearly or subtly that I'm not the right type of something. Maybe you, too, have been attacked for not conforming to someone else's understanding of a particular role. The assumption underlying the attack is that you aren't the right _____. You aren't . . .

- the right type of boss. Because the right type of boss pays for the first round of drinks . . . and you don't go out drinking with the crew.

- the right type of administrator. The right type of administrator attends all the team meetings . . . instead of just *some* meetings.

- the right type of friend. The right type of friend agrees all the time . . . instead of having open, honest conversations.

- the right type of family member. The right type of family member keeps the family secrets . . . instead of trying to change patterns.

- the right type of leader. The right type of leader knows everyone's names, makes the right calls always, is commanding but sincere, and wields a magic wand to solve all personnel conflicts.

- the right type of Christian. The right type of Christian takes a chastity vow, never swears, and trusts that God has a plan. Or is it that the right type of Christian marches in protests, disregards piety as a work of the law, and scoffs at religious platitudes?

The lie that we must be the right type of _____ abounds. Like its fellow impostors, this lie can subtly influence our behavior as we strive, in ways that may not be authentic, to increase our chances of being accepted, liked, safe, or free of others' judgment. We absorb the lie's cues through the social context. The problem is that what constitutes the right type of boss, pastor, administrator, teacher, friend, coworker *changes* as the social context changes—with the situation and larger cultural norms.

For example, when I was a young pastor, it seemed that being flexible, accommodating, and going above and beyond to help others was a cultural norm for people in church work. Now I notice when coaching new clergy that they have more awareness of the need to set boundaries and to take care of self—and a sense of power to do these things. Now I also see that both going above and beyond *and* setting good boundaries have great merit. In leadership we need to exercise both flexibility *and* Sabbath-keeping. Our ministries benefit when we are accommodating toward our parishioners and colleagues for the sake of the larger mission *and* when we take care of ourselves. But my understanding of what it means to be the "right" type of pastor has changed as our context has changed.

Furthermore, "the right type of _____" is often in the eye of the beholder. For example, my ideal boss, or leader, might have different characteristics from yours. My administrator at the care center has been a wonderful supervisor for me because he allows me to work with a large amount of autonomy. This is how I work best. He trusts me to do my job, and I take that trust seriously. I often approach him with an idea for a new initiative, I present the plan, and he usually says, "Go for it." I then go and do it and come back to him if I need additional resources. This type of supervision allows me to do my best work, but it may be too hands-off for someone else.

The lie that we're not the right type of _____ chips away at our capacity to bounce back by planting seeds of self-doubt. It drives the question, "What if they're right? What if I really am a fraud? What if I'm really not who I present myself to be?" and, worse yet, "What if they can see something in me that I can't, and I'm really not who *I* think I am?" This lie makes us believe that our best options are to pretend and hide.

The claim that I'm not the right type of _____ often comes up around faith—that I'm not Christian *enough*, that I don't believe the right things, and that my faith in Jesus Christ is less than someone else's. I knew I wasn't the right type of pastor (and by implication, the right type of Christian) for the octogenarian to whom I served lunch one day at the care center. He made it very clear. I hadn't yet met this gentleman, who was apparently there to recover and then head home. I introduced myself: "Hello, I'm Chaplain Sarah. I'll be helping with lunch today."

He jumped in: "You're a what?"

The way he said "what" put my limbic system on high alert and sent out the call "Man the battle stations!"

"I'm a leavin'," I thought. That's a what.

But instead I responded, "I'm a chaplain here. I'm Chaplain Sarah."

After knowing me for about thirty-eight seconds, he summed up my professional offering to the world and me with these words: "You shouldn't be a chaplain. You should be a helpmate."

I should be a *what*?

This took my breath away. And not in a good way.

Writing this, I feel like I *should* say that I had the calm of Mother Teresa and his comment didn't hurt me, that I could look on him with amused, magnanimous delight as a fellow broken child of God. That would be a version of myself you could more easily admire or love. But that would be a steamin', heapin' pile of hooey. Before I could get close to feeling kindness in my heart for him, I'd need to vent and get judge-y myself, because there are times when, as a woman in ministry, I feel like I've been punched in the gut. For him, I wasn't the right type of Christian, because the right type of Christian *woman* is one who helps her husband, is submissive to men, and probably doesn't speak in church. While he lobbed Genesis 3 at me, he overlooked other biblical passages that show women in leadership—women like Deborah, Priscilla, Shiphrah, and Puah—weighty biblical contradictions to his assertion. It seemed he was accustomed to wielding cultural power in his Christian faith. He seemed to think that because he was older and a man, he could level his judgment at me.

When I tell this story, I'm often asked what I did. Some people hope I was quick-witted and offered an assertive, yet playful, response. Unfortunately, I'm just not that quick on my feet when I'm in an amygdala hijack. Others want to hear that I called him out. I have fantasized about what that would have looked like. In the more elaborate visions, I have a cape with the initials STC ("Super Theological Corrector") on the back, and I give out pamphlets with titles like "Winning Souls Back from Misogyny" and "5

Easy Steps to Navigate Mean-Spiritedness from Brothers and Sisters of the Faith."

But I had no cape, nor pamphlets—only his baked fish and rice pilaf in hand.

"Well, let me help you get your food."

Fulfilling the role he imagined I was best at, I arranged the food in front of him and asked if there was anything else I could get him, knowing these actions reinforced the belief that women should serve men. It would have been inappropriate in this context for me to call him out for his theology. It would have been beyond my role to even invite him into a new understanding that, as the resident bill of rights states, you can practice your religion free of harassment. If for him, that practice of religion meant freely handing out judgments on other people about how they should live their faith, so be it.

I imagine if we had met in a different setting, one in which he didn't feel worried about his progress in physical therapy or scared he wouldn't be able to return home, our brief exchange might have been more pleasant. I know my best self doesn't show up when I'm sick and worried.

Unfortunately, this incident isn't an isolated one. I cannot tell you how many times I have watched someone's demeanor visibly change when I reveal not that I'm the wrong *type* of Christian but that I'm a Christian (or pastor) at all. Shoulders tighten, smiles fade, lips become lines, words dry up to a trickle. When I was part of an international exchange program with young adults from around the world, I had a conversation with a free-spirited guy from Australia. When I told him I was a seminary student studying to be a pastor, he literally got up, walked away, and didn't give me more than a terse greeting for the rest of the two-month program. Sometimes I feel caught up in knots someone else tied.

What had been his experience with pastors or Christianity before that time when openly rejecting someone on a program designed to *foster goodwill* felt like his best choice? Had he had an off-putting experience of being judged unfairly by someone using the Bible? Had he heard someone else be shamed or belittled because they didn't believe or practice the right thing? Had he had an experience similar to what I heard one snowy wintry morning?

Pulling out of my garage, I had started out listening to NPR, subconsciously hoping for some good news but, of course, hearing depressing information about how the planet will be uninhabitable sooner than we had thought. I started flipping. The pop station had some inane call-in going on about what to do when you find the profile of the spouse of a college friend on Tinder. Do you swipe right? Do you tell your friend whom you haven't spoken to for twelve years and with whom you only exchange thumbs-up on social media that their spouse is wayward? Do you leave it alone?

This is the stuff we divert ourselves with so we don't have to think about the demise of the planet. Ugh, the disintegration of society! While hanging in with the relationship drama would have given me a good opportunity to reflect on social interactions and morals, it was too much for my drive. Flip again. The country station was playing new country, songs I didn't know. I needed some vintage "Fishin' in the Dark" and "Calling Baton Rouge" to get me going. More retro Garth Brooks, Reba, or Alabama.

I decided to give the Christian station a try.

When I tuned in, the host was saying, "Maybe like me, you are trying to live into your New Year's resolution to be less of a people-pleaser. I want to work on being more selfish and not saying yes to everything and then being resentful."

Oh, buddy, I see this getting worse for you before it gets better. You just said "be more selfish" on a Christian radio station. That might work over in the Tinder-swipe conversation, but here, this isn't going to go unnoticed. I advise you phone a friend.

The first caller, a woman, came on the air and said, "I'm calling to speak the truth in love." As soon as I heard those words from Ephesians, my stomach tightened and I was glad I wasn't on the receiving end of this call. "Speaking the truth in love" at times by some Christians is used as the biblical golden ticket to render judgment or point out someone's flaws or failings in a very direct, blunt way.

The caller got right to the point. "Nowhere in the Bible does it say we should be selfish. Selfishness is a sin, and we are to give ourselves away in love."

Called out. Biblical smackdown. Right there for all to hear. The radio announcer wasn't the right type of Christian.

I shoulda stuck with the Tinder swiping.

This radio announcer was being vulnerable, sharing a bit about his struggles with boundaries, asking others to relate to their own stories of struggle, with the intent, I believe, to be healthier people. The radio host said, "I guess what I'm trying to say is, I want to find more balance in my life."

The caller connected with this. "Oh, that is fine. Jesus sought balance when he needed rest from the crowds and went away by himself to pray." The opening chords of "Lion of Judah" started softly in the background, and the conversation came to a close.

Now, I know I run the risk of being judgmental about the judgment of this caller. But your judgment of my judgment of her judgment is a risk I'll take for the lesson. Yes, the truth needs to be spoken and heard, but *how* we speak it impacts *how* it is heard. If I've spoken the truth in love and then feel superior to you instead of feeling connected through our mutual human habit of missing the mark at times, then I haven't spoken the truth in love. I've spoken the truth in self-righteousness, which is completely opposed to love. If I am gloating about your exposed failure, secretly excited to see the fallout, I haven't spoken the truth in love. I've spoken the truth, perhaps, but in superiority. Truth spoken without kindness, humility, and curiosity can be mean-spirited, even cruel, with the consequence—intentional or unintentional—of shutting down the other person so they are unlikely to grow in spirit and heart.

(Oh, and by the way, the word *balance* for emotional health isn't biblical, either. Just sayin'.)

Did you see that?! I just did it! I just did the exact same thing the caller did. When I wrote that *balance* for emotional health isn't a biblical word, I felt superior. Because the caller isn't the right type of Christian for me, I felt the glee of judging the judge-y caller and catching her in her own trap! We all have blind spots a mile wide.

Oh, my sin is ever before me, and let it be so, Lord.

Finding My Way to Truth: Authenticity

I get sucked into the lie that someone should be the right type of _____. Time and time again, when with my non-churchgoing friends I have judged other Christians, like the radio show caller, who have turned my friends off of organized religion. But in those moments, I'm not speaking the truth in love. I'm simply bad-mouthing my own people to show I'm not like that—I'm not one of *those* Christians. Because the cold, hard truth is that I've been hurt by other Christians; I've been judged by *those* Christians.

Pay Attention

These judgments about not being Christian enough or the right type really sucked the wind out of me a few years ago, and I had to really work this process of "pay attention, examine, and apply the learning." It was one of the hardest experiences I've ever had to grapple with. Someone with power over me made a very painful decision that impacted and will forever impact many mutual relationships because his decision is now part of our common story. Because of this person's pressure and influence, I was disinvited from leading a large gathering and was replaced with a male clergyperson from a more conservative denomination. The one with power-over felt so strongly that I should not be involved in the event that he told the organizers that he would not attend if I was leading.

This took my breath away. And not in a good way.

Oh, my God. Sometimes all you can say is "Oh, my God." In the same moment it is a prayer and a swear.

What was my response to the news of the disinvite? What did I need to pay attention to? Here is some of what was happening to me physically, mentally, and emotionally.

Physically: When I first learned the news of the disinvite, I went numb, which actually made it possible for me to attend the meeting I was en route to. I felt nothing, and other than being quieter than usual in this meeting, there was no outward indication anything was wrong. Then, when I called my husband, I cried and cried. I felt so hurt, disrespected, rejected, and disregarded—hard emotions that leeched away my physical energy. When I got home, I went to bed very early because I was spent, and I knew that going over the events again wouldn't be productive. I knew from experience that no good would come from staying up.

Mentally: Initially, I couldn't get my thoughts off the idea that maybe he was right. My mind looped with thoughts like: *Maybe I'm not fit to be a pastor. Maybe I am a fraud. Maybe I am a fake. I'm not good enough, pious enough, humble enough, kind enough, forgiving enough, churchy enough. I do like to swear a bit every now and again. Maybe I am a pastor impostor, somehow fooling everyone, from bishops to congregants, and even God.* But finally, this fellow had caught me and seen through my guise. And if I wasn't disinvited because I wasn't the right type of Christian, then what was the reason? How deeply did he despise me?

Emotionally: Initially, my emotions were numb, then they were a flood of grief, resentment, anger, and shame. Shame loves to keep us perseverating on *one* experience as the *whole* truth. In these moments, I couldn't remember or grab onto all of the affirmations I'd received for my ministry from care center residents and colleagues. I couldn't see what was right in front of me every Wednesday and Sunday—a chapel of elders from at least eight denominations across the spectrum from very conservative to very liberal. And in twelve years I hadn't heard anyone say they thought I was faking it. Instead, they often graciously affirmed my ministry with words like "The love of Christ shines in your words."

Yet even weeks later, I still couldn't talk about this incident without weeping, and I felt so hated. I didn't know anyone else who had had this experience. I tried not to spend too much time feeling angry, because I knew from my experiences at Bethlehem Acres and the church I had served that anger masks pain; it doesn't make it go away.

In the midst of feeling my way through the emotional fallout of the disinvite, I called one of my dearest friends from seminary, Lace. I cried, "Am I a fake Christian? Maybe I'm not fit to be a pastor."

The power of this judgment had started to chip away at my groundedness and to replace it with an abiding sadness.

Lace said, "You are the most loving, generous person I know."

But I needed to hear more. "Tell me I am called to be a pastor," I said.

"You are called to be a pastor."

Receiving this type of support helped calm my mind so over the course of a few weeks I could ask myself, "What can I learn in this and from this experience so I am more whole, more integrated, more authentic?" I sheepishly uncovered the fact that I hadn't shared stories of my faith with this power broker. I had debated theology, but depending on the environment, that can be vastly different from telling personal stories of what God has done in one's life. Some people love debating and arguing the nuances of something like reading the Old Testament through the lens of Christ; it gives them a thrill like no other. That isn't me. The sobering fact is, I had forgotten this truth about myself the last time I was with the power broker (before the disinvite). I had been trying to make a connection, and at first, I felt like little bridges of connection were being built. Yet, as the conversation went on, it felt less like bridge-building and more like theological ambush as I was talked over, interrupted, pontificated to, and accused.

Examine

I decided to dig into learning more about how my lifelong tendency of people-pleasing had played out in this situation, because I suspected it had not served me well. I had kowtowed too quickly to what I *thought* would make others comfortable; I hadn't shared my stories of faith. With this power broker, I was trying to avoid being judged as "too churchy" or as one who "thinks she's better than us." I wasn't too keen on more people literally walking away from me, like the free-spirited Aussie had done. After all, there is only so much judgment a person can take. Thus, I was too accommodating. This was tiring for me, yet almost second nature—a skill I had learned at a young age. For instance, I remember making brownies with my grandma once, and she asked if I liked nuts in my brownies. At six, I knew I didn't, but I said, "Do *you* like nuts in your brownies?" She said yes. Well, that sealed the deal for me—then I liked nuts too!

I needed to dig into what was behind the behavior of accommodation. I had to get curious, and in doing so, I realized my *own judgment.* I didn't want to be like "those Christians" or be labeled "one of those Christians." I didn't want to be perceived as pushy or overbearing, or as a know-it-all, or as small-minded and judgmental. I didn't want to floodlight someone so they didn't feel heard or seen in God's grace but instead felt shut out by my words and how I delivered them. In my years of chaplaincy, I have heard hundreds of stories of how Christians and the church have shamed, belittled, and hurt people. Because I never want to further that pain, I had stayed so clear of these negatives that I didn't speak as authentically as I truly wanted to about my faith.

After examining the disinvite, sitting with the pain, and

gleaning what I could learn from it, I committed to sharing my faith when it felt authentic to do so.

This was top of mind when I got the invitation to be on a podcast, a professional dream of mine. As the event got closer, I put together my notes and jotted down stories to illustrate my understanding of what it means to be a healer—the topic of the podcast. Therapists were the usual guests; a pastor had never been on this podcast. Even though my friend and colleague was the host, I knew this conversation would challenge my new practice of being mindfully authentic in my faith. I would be respectful, open, and kind, certainly, and truthful and honest to my own story.

During the interview I spoke spontaneously about my theological understanding of confession and shared my interpretation of the end of John's Gospel. I delighted in talking about Jesus creating safe space for Peter to acknowledge his brokenness and pain and to move through it to emotional integration so that he could serve and lead others well. I was on a roll; I was having fun! I was enjoying sharing insights that had been powerful for me. I readily spoke about how church has hurt and wounded people, but I also spoke about how some people have been called "beloved" there, having never heard that before.

Then it got really real. While I thought I was steering clear of anxiety-producing church-related topics—judgment and hell, for example—my friend vulnerably and honestly shared that the words "Bible" and "Jesus" were causing small walls of protection to go up in her heart; she was noticing these words were triggering her.

Immediately, I thought, "Oh no! I want to be authentic, not put someone in a worse space than when I started speaking." Maybe this is the very problem with trying to live an authentic faith in a complicated world; my authenticity may be someone else's trigger. That is exactly what I was trying to avoid all along. I didn't want to be *one of those Christians*—one who did more harm than good. And it looked like in that moment I was skirting very close to that.

Even though I became much less articulate and all sorts of lies were whispering in my ear ("Look! You've made a mistake! You crossed a line you shouldn't have! You can't win for trying."), I later learned that the host had her own variations of "I've done something wrong" swirling in her thoughts. And yet disconnection and fear weren't going to own this conversation. She wasn't asking me to stop saying my church words, and I wasn't asking her to move to an emotional place of accepting them as life-giving. Neither of us needed the other to change. When I listened to the podcast, I'm proud of how we stayed in the hard, uncomfortable—but authentic—space of having two things be true at the same time.

Apply the Learning

Living an authentic faith isn't an easy binary of either/or: either do share or don't share; either call in to the radio show and offer correction or assume the radio host used the wrong word and let it go. What would I need to know to make a more grounded, authentic decision the next time I felt the share/don't share tension? This is what I came up with:

1. *Know the context:* In this podcast, the driving question for all the interviews was "How do you understand yourself as a healer?" This question set the context for what I shared. I can talk about how my work as a chaplain and coach is built on my Christian faith, but that doesn't mean I don't value hearing about someone's Muslim faith or

Jewish faith, especially in these polarizing times, or how you've been hurt by the church and can't go back. I want to understand diverse experiences and perspectives. My decision to attend to the context—in this case, to authentically respond to the podcast question—means I shared my story wholly and completely, and I learned to trust that if discomfort emerges, together with respect and kindness, we can stay in and learn from the discomfort.

2. *Know my role:* Am I a person with historical power in this relationship? If so, then I need to listen more than talk. Am I serving as a facilitator in this conversation? If so, then my role is to ask questions to elicit growth and to help you develop deeper understanding about yourself. Am I the only person here who is a pastor or am I among other church professionals? Am I the only person here who is a churchgoer? Ultimately, though, no matter what my role, I need to remember that what I say, how I say it, and why I say it are important, because the other has a story about Christians, Christianity, and the church too, and I want to represent my faith and the church well.

3. *Be grounded:* Am I saying things I believe to be true? Am I saying things that need to be said by me, and now? (Thank you, AA, for this universally applicable question.) Am I saying things that are life-giving and true? Am I calm? Do I feel connected and grounded through prayer to God? Am I not already angry, upset, or anxious? Have I discerned what is my responsibility and what is not? Initially, I felt bad about the podcast trigger warning, but once I got grounded through journaling, I realized that I didn't need to feel bad. Feeling bad wasn't mine to carry. The podcast host knew her audience, and by adding a trigger warning, she served her community and me as a guest well, because then listeners could make an informed choice about whether to listen.

4. *Know myself:* Honestly, I don't know if I'm the right type of Christian. Oh, yes, there are many moments when I know God's worked through me and I've been directed by the Spirit. Some moments in ministry make my heart sing and clearly show both me and the person I'm with that my love is from God—that my heart is open. I've experienced moments in preaching when I'm moved to tears because the truth of God's love is still so real and profound—moments when I've witnessed incredible growth, healing, and new life.

There are also days and moments when my faith seems more of a cognitive assent than a living embodiment of God's grace. Days when I know the "right" answers, but they feel hollow. Days when I wonder, *What is God doing? Where is God when so many know only suffering?* Days when I know the response to this theodicy question is that as a follower of Jesus, I'm supposed to get to work addressing suffering. And then days when *that* thought makes me want to live in blissful ignorance, or just go back to bed in defeat. Days when I look at my fellow Christians and wonder how we can possibly be of the same tribe.

And then there is me. I have enough blind spots and self-deceptions to fill a room. I can judge other Christians out of self-defense. I've forgotten most of the Greek I learned in seminary, and if I had to save my family from a sinking ship, securing places on a lifeboat by reciting hours of Bible verses from memory, quoting chapter and verse, they'd better start swimming. If that means I'm not the right type of Christian in someone's mind, then, for them, maybe I'm not.

Yet, in the end, none of us who follow Christ are Christian enough or the right type of Christian . . . which is what makes us Christian. I am not a Christian because of my words or deeds, my actions or inactions. I am a

Christian because in my baptism, God said I am. My duty and delight are to live into that calling devotedly, humbly, and authentically.

May *that* take my breath away. In a good way.

9.

An Invitation

Long before I knew who I "should" be or what might make me seem "most likable" or impressive to others; long before I had a sense that I should shape myself into who I thought others would like me to be; long before I understood how the lies I told myself could contort my thinking and behavior—my older brother and I trotted along after our dad on the farm. He strode across the farmyard, and I scampered behind, three of my steps for every one of Dad's. While our dad fixed a tractor or baler, or fed the pigs, he often whistled.

Try as I might, I hadn't yet mastered whistling, but I'd often sing little bits of songs from Sunday school or a simple tune that landed in my head. When I was older, one of my jobs was hanging clothes on the line, and I'd sing a song I was composing as the words and tune came together. Or I'd preach to the blackbirds who perched in the shelter belt of Russian olive trees my father had planted decades before. Both the singing and the preaching felt so true and right in my child's heart.

At times I was moved to tears by what I felt and by the words that came to me. I knew that God's love was as wide as the blue prairie sky spread beyond the sheets and towels snapping in the wind. Now I think that part of our journey to authenticity is to return to the truth of the callings we felt when we were too young to turn on the stove, but wise and attentive enough to know what made our hearts sing.

Five years ago, I was attending training for a leadership position within a national organization. Those of us in the leadership track were given the opportunity at the end of the training to introduce ourselves and share a little bit about our professional focus with 125 new candidates who had just completed their first step in the training. The candidates' next step would be to select one of us as a partner for individual consultation.

Some of the lies we've been looking at together in this book showed up as I was preparing what to say. I wanted to be impressive and prove that a mistake hadn't been made when I was asked to take on this new position. I was the only pastor among therapists and coaches who would be introduced, and that also drove a little bit of my thinking: "I have to be the right type of Christian."

Even though these lies were still calling me away from my authenticity, I had been writing a song during the three days of training. Phrases of it came to me in the evenings when I was reflecting on the amazing moments of the day, or when I was out for a run on a late afternoon break. The bits of song seemed to say, "Those lies are wrong," and to ask, "What would happen if, in my introduction, I showed up as my authentic self and let my heart's song be my introduction?"

The next morning, surrounded by the other twelve case consultants (whom I had fallen in love with because of the depth of all we'd shared with each other), I sang my song, and they danced and clapped in support. My voice quivered in the beginning, but it didn't matter.

I got invited to the ball,
But I'm not gonna play it small,
I know I've got a lot to give,
So, I'm gonna dance.
I'm gonna dance.
I'm gonna dance.

I'm twirlin' around the room,
My heart is startin' to bloom,
I'm singing for the joy,
Yeah! I love to dance.
I love to dance.
I love to dance.

It's a gift to be alive,
But I hoard, thieve, and hide.
Am I enough to do this dance?
I've . . . gotta take a chance.
Gotta take a chance.
Gotta take a chance.

Here's the thing you've got to know;
It's food for your starving soul:
When you say yes! you can only grow,
'Cuz . . . you're invited too.
You're invited too.
You're invited too.

People started singing along, some stood up to dance along, and there was clapping. It was a moment of joy that I got to invite others into. I brought my whole authentic self. But this sense of connection to others and to my truest self was short-lived. As I sat back down, those lies I know so well slithered up to me and said, "I've been a show-off, and people must think I think I'm special, and it was stupid." By the time we broke for lunch, I felt almost ashamed of what I'd done. As the room was clearing, a mentor of mine came up and hugged me. I told her how I felt like it was a mistake, and what *had* I done, and people thought it was stupid. I'll never forget what she said. She said, "People clapped along, they were loving it, you saw that. And you were being brave."

When we commit to leading from our hearts and living more authentically, these lies don't go away, but we'll see them faster. And when they still feel like truth, I pray someone comes along and says to you, "You were being brave."

In my leading, parenting, loving, and living, *I'm gonna dance.*

And you're invited too.